STEVENS
Institute of Technology

Post-Quantum Cryptography Using Complexity
Doctoral Dissertation

Michael de Mare
Department of Computer Science
Stevens Institute of Technology
1 Castle Point on Hudson
Hoboken, NJ 07030

mdemare@cs.stevens.edu

Committee
Rebecca N. Wright
Stephen L. Bloom
Susanne Wetzel
Robert Gilman
Josh Benaloh

PhD Defense Version February 27, 2009.

Post-Quantum Cryptography Using Complexity

by

Michael James de Mare

A DISSERTATION

Submitted to the Faculty of the Stevens Institute of Technology in partial fulfillment of the requirements for the degree of

DOCTOR OF PHILOSOPHY

Michael de Mare, Candidate	Date

<u>ADVISORY COMMITTEE</u>

Rebecca N. Wright, co-chair	Date

Stephen L. Bloom, co-chair	Date

Susanne Wetzel	Date

Robert Gilman	Date

Josh Benaloh	Date

STEVENS INSTITUTE OF TECHNOLOGY
Castle Point on Hudson
Hoboken, NJ 07030
2008

POST-QUANTUM CRYPTOGRAPHY USING COMPLEXITY

ABSTRACT

In order to cope with new technologies such as quantum computing and the possibility of developing new algorithms, new cryptosystems should be developed based on a diverse set of unrelated complexity assumptions so that one technique will not break more than a handful of systems. As demonstrated by Shor in 1994, quantum algorithms are known to break traditional cryptosystems based on RSA and Diffie-Hellman. Therefore, post-quantum systems are needed to provide security should quantum computers become a reality.

In this thesis, we develop two post-quantum cryptographic primitives: a symmetric-key cipher using two new cipher design techniques and a solution to the secure set membership problem. The new techniques in the symmetric-key cipher are polymorphic S-boxes and pseudo-independent subkeys. The secure set membership primitive includes a distributed protocol for set establishment and a proof-of-possession protocol to show set membership without revealing the member of the set.

The symmetric-key cipher is based on state-of-the-art cipher designs along with our new cipher design techniques. This makes its base properties predictable while adding what we believe to be new difficulties for the cryptanalyst. The polymorphic S-box technique may be used with new ciphers while existing ciphers may be retrofitted to use pseudo-independent subkeys.

We use a subset of the instances of the 3SAT witness-finding problem in developing a new complexity assumption for the secure set membership primitive. It is risky to base cryptosystems on NP-complete problems, as what is hard in the worst case may be easy in most cases. To mitigate this risk, we limit the instances of 3SAT that we generate to try to select only hard instances; our complexity assumption is different than mere *NP*-completeness.

Author: Michael de Mare

Adviser: Rebecca N. Wright

Date: November 7, 2008

Department: Computer Science

Degree: Doctor of Philosophy

Acknowledgments

I would first and foremost like to thank my adviser, Rebecca Wright, without whom there would be no thesis. Her guidance and comments are what made this possible. I also appreciate her close readings of the drafts and comments that made the thesis what it is. I would also like to thank the rest of my committee, Stephen Bloom, Susanne Wetzel, Robert Gilman, and Josh Benaloh for their time and assistance. I would like to particularly thank Rebecca Wright and Robert Gilman for funding the research and development of this thesis. I would additionally like to thank Josh Benaloh for serving as my mentor, encouraging me to go to graduate school, providing guidance on where to go, and making it possible for me to attend Stevens.

I would like to thank my colleagues in my adviser's Tuesday afternoon meetings, Rebecca Wright, Vijay Ramachandran, Sotiris Ioannidis, Mike Engling, Onur Kardes, and Geetha Jagannathan for both their presentations and for listening to mine as well as their helpful comments. I would like to thank the members of the Laboratory for Secure Systems and the Algebraic Cryptography Center for listening to my work and offering their suggestions and comments.

I would like to thank the people with whom I spoke with at conferences and workshops, too numerous to mention, who asked insightful questions and provided helpful information. I would like to thank Whit Diffie for his comments on symmetric-key ciphers and Lincoln Decoursey for help running experiments.

I would like to thank my parents for their (sometimes financial) support. I would particularly like to thank my mother for proofreading drafts of my thesis. This wouldn't have been possible without them.

Contents

1 Introduction   1

2 Related Work   5
   2.1 Limits of Complexity-based Cryptography   6
        2.1.1 One-way Permutations are Not NP-hard to Invert   7
        2.1.2 Generic Complexity   9
   2.2 The Quantum Adversary   10
   2.3 Proposed Post-Quantum Systems   13
   2.4 Ciphers   17

3 Definitions and Models of Computation   24
   3.1 Block Ciphers 24
   3.2 Turing Machines   26
   3.3 Complexity Classes   28
   3.4 Oracle Notation 30
   3.5 Zero Knowledge 30

4 Dragonfire: A Cipher With Polymorphic S-boxes   31
   4.1 Complexity of Symmetric-Key Ciphers   35
   4.2 General Design   36
   4.3 Cryptanalytic Attacks   40
   4.4 The Pineapple Cipher   42
        4.4.1 Design 43
        4.4.2 Security 47
        4.4.3 Performance 52
   4.5 Dragonfire Cipher   58
   4.6 Pseudorandom Number Generator   69
   4.7 Discussion   72

5 Secure Set Membership Using 3SAT   74
   5.1 Related Work   77
   5.2 Preliminaries   79
   5.3 Secure Set Membership   81

5.3.1   Centralized Set Establishment Protocol 81
5.3.2   Distributed Set Establishment Protocol 85
5.3.3   Set Membership 91
5.3.4   Security 92
5.4   Applications 98
5.4.1   Digital Credentials 98
5.4.2   Accounts with multiple users 98
5.4.3   Access Control Lists 99
5.4.4   Document timestamping 99
5.5   Discussion 101

6   Conclusion   104

List of Tables

Top Disagreeing Bits for Pineapple 48
Top Agreeing Bits for Pineapple 49
Avalanche experiment results 55
Differential analysis results for Pineapple 56
Top 2-bit Differential Results 57
Results from NIST tests on Dragonfire PRNG 71

List of Figures

Grover's Algorithm 12
Evolution of Block Ciphers 19

Overview of an iterated cipher 38
Feistel cipher design 39
f-function for Pineapple and Dragonfire 46
Polymorphic S-box selection 60
S-box generation for Dragonfire 61
Dragonfire key scheduling 63
Subkeys not determined by same bits 68
Subkeys determined by same bits 69

Values of *maxreject* for $\ell = 128, n = 1024, m = 50$ 90
Highest experimental rejections for $\ell = 128, n = 1024, m = 50$ 90

Chapter 1

Introduction

In order to cope with new technologies such as quantum computing and the possibility of developing new algorithms, new cryptosystems should be developed based on a diverse set of unrelated complexity assumptions so that one technique will not break more than a handful of systems.

Quantum computers, if built, will exploit physical properties to efficiently factor and compute discrete logarithms [Sho94]. We say that a cryptographic system is *post-quantum* if there is no known efficient algorithm for a quantum computer to break it. With physicists performing quantum calculations using one or two qubit systems and promising full quantum computers in fifteen to twenty-five years, it is time to develop cryptographic systems that are resilient against quantum attack. While we hope to make systems resistant to quantum algorithms, no proof methods are known to show a system resistant to quantum attack.

This thesis presents cryptographic systems that seem to be resilient to quantum attacks including a primitive protocol based on an NP-hard problem. While there is no proof that quantum computers cannot solve NP-hard problems efficiently, there is a relativized lower bound for NP that is as strong as the similar evidence for classical computers [BBBV97]. Our systems include both symmetric-key ciphers and a primitive to solve the set membership problem.

We present a cryptographic primitive which while not asymptotically complex is believed to have a large enough work factor to make it impractical to break for either state-of-the-art classical or near-future quantum computers. If either type of computer can decide *NP* efficiently, though, it can break this system. Our cryptographic primitive is a block cipher incorporating two methods new in this thesis.

The cryptographic primitive based on an *NP*-complete problem solves the secure set membership problem, which we also define. The secure set membership problem is the problem of representing a set in such a way that it is easy to verify membership in the set but hard to find a member of the set. Our proposed solution includes a secure distributed protocol for establishing the set.

It is risky to base the security of cryptographic systems on *NP*-complete problems simply because they are *NP*-complete because what is hard in the worst case may not be hard in the average case. For this reason, attention must be paid to the actual complexity assumption used, as it is subtly different than simple *NP*-completeness. To introduce complexity, in Chapter 2 we discuss complexity results for cryptography, as well as the quantum adversary, other post-quantum systems, and the evolution of block ciphers.

Chapter 4 introduces the two new techniques for the design of symmetric-key ciphers and a cipher that implements them. While current symmetric-key cipher technology seems secure with the adoption of Rijndael as the Advanced Encryption Standard, the Iranians had access to the same literature as the Rijndael designers and we have learned that their cipher was broken [RJ04, Coc07]. For this reason, it seems prudent to develop new techniques to enhance the security of block ciphers. Our new cipher, called Dragonfire, can also be used as a secure pseudorandom number generator for protocols developed in this thesis.

Our cipher provides the building blocks needed to practically implement the results of Chapter 5, which describes the secure set membership problem and proposes a solution to it based on the well known 3SAT problem. The secure set membership problem is a generalization of the problem solved by one-way accumulators [BdM94] of verifying that a string is a member of a predetermined set; our solution has the advantages of not relying on problems that are known to be broken by quantum computers as the implementation of one-way accumulators do and of not requiring a second string to be remembered. Another implementation of one-way accumulators using bilinear pairing [Ngu05] can also be broken by quantum computers [MOV93]. This is because the discrete logarithm problem can be solved by quantum computers [Sho94]. We believe that both of our systems are secure under the quantum model if they are secure under the classical model.

The Dragonfire cipher introduced in Chapter 4 contains two new methods in cipher design. These new techniques have broad applicability in the design of new symmetric-key ciphers.

A preliminary version of the work in Chapter 5 appeared at the Eighth International Conference on Information and Communications Security [dMW06]. We introduce the problem of secure set membership and provide a candidate post-quantum solution for it.

Our contribution, in summary, is that we:

- Introduce polymorphic S-boxes as a symmetric cipher technique.

- Introduce pseudo-independent subkeys as a symmetric cipher technique.

- Define the secure set-membership problem.

- Propose a method to solve the secure set membership problem using a trusted central authority.

- Propose a method to solve the secure set membership problem using a group of authorities who are not individually trusted.

Chapter 2

Related Work

Work related to this thesis includes theoretical efforts to understand the relationship between *NP*-hardness and cryptography, the quantum adversary, post-quantum systems, and other symmetric-key ciphers. We discuss this work in order to allow us to understand what the limits of we might accomplish, the model of computation for an adversary, and what has already been done in the field. Additional related work will be discussed in each chapter.

In Section 2.1 of this chapter, we explore what can be accomplished with complexity-based cryptography by first examining a result showing that one-way permutations that are *NP*-complete to invert are not likely to exist. *NP* deals with decision problems, so we abuse the idea of *NP*-completeness to describe a one-way function as *NP*-hard or *NP*-complete to invert. In Subsection 2.1.2 we examine a method of determining the "usual" complexity of a problem. We then examine the capabilities of an adversary equipped with a quantum computer. In Section 2.3, we survey a sample of proposed post-quantum cryptosystems. Post-quantum systems should be resistant to attack by an adversary equipped with a quantum computer.

In the last section, we discuss proposed symmetric-key ciphers that we considered when designing the Pineapple and Dragonfire ciphers in Chapter 4. The list of ciphers discussed is by no means comprehensive.

2.1 Limits of Complexity-based Cryptography

We say that a cryptographic system is *complexity-based* if its security is derived from the belief that breaking it will lead to an efficient algorithm for a complexity class that is believed difficult. In that spirit, when we say that a one-way function is *NP*-hard to invert, we mean that given an oracle that inverts it, a deterministic Turing Machine can decide an *NP*-complete problem in polynomial time. If inverting the function is *NP*-hard and can be written as a decision problem in *NP*, then we say that the function is *NP*-complete to invert. In this section, we discuss limits to what can be accomplished with complexity-based cryptography. Subsection 2.1.1 shows that there exists a function computed by a polynomial-time bounded deterministic Turing machine with an oracle that inverts a one-way permutation, $P^{f^{-1}}$, where f is a one-way permutation, that is in $NP \cap coNP$ [Bra79]. Assuming, as is commonly believed, that $NP \neq coNP$, this means that a cipher cannot be *NP*-hard to invert. For this reason, in Chapter 5, we propose a function that is weaker than a one-way permutation and is strongly related to an *NP*-hard problem. This function is likely the most powerful function based on complexity possible because of Brassard's theorem [Bra79]. We also discuss another problem with complexity-based cryptography. That problem is that while complexity classes are based on *worst-case* complexity, cryptography requires that all but an asymptotically negligible number of instances be hard.

2.1.1 One-way Permutations are Not *NP*-hard to Invert

We start with a 1979 result by Brassard that suggests that basing cryptography on *NP*-hardness may be futile [Bra79]. Specifically, Brassard shows that if any one-to-one one-way function whose input size is bounded on the size of the output is *NP*-hard to invert, then $NP = coNP$. It follows that one-way permutations cannot be shown *NP*-complete under the usual assumptions. For this result, the domain (which is a set of strings—i.e., a language) of the one-way function must be in *NP* and the range (also a language) of the one-way function must be in *coNP*. When the domain of the function is *NP*; a Turing machine must be able to decide in nondeterministic polynomial time if an input is valid for the function. In most cases, where any string is a valid input, this is trivially true.

Brassard does not show this result directly, but rather shows a specific result for the discrete logarithm problem and sketches it for factoring, simply stating that it generalizes. It is worthwhile to take the time to understand how the generalization works because this is fundamental to understanding the computational complexity of breaking cryptographic systems. The domain of a one-way function is a binary string that can be interpreted as an integer. The decision problem is specified as follows: Given y, t such that $f(x) = y$, is $x > t$? Brassard's result is that this problem is in *coNP*. In order to show this, he must show that there is a succinct witness that there is no x such that $x > t$. Since the function is one-to-one, it is sufficient to show that there exists an x' such that $f(x') = y$ and $x' \leq t$. This x' serves as a witness that there is no x such that $f(x) = y$ and $x > t$ by the pigeonhole principle. Therefore this problem is in *coNP*. Brassard goes on to show that if an *NP*-complete problem is in *coNP*, then *NP=coNP*.

Note that Brassard's result only applies to functions that are one-to-one. In contrast, Kozen showed a simple example of a one-way function that is not one-to-one but is *NP*-hard to invert [Koz06]. One-to-one one-way functions are known as *one-way permutations*. Impagliazzo and Rudich showed that if $P \neq NP$ then one-way permutations cannot be used as black boxes for stronger cryptographic primitives such as key agreement [Rud88, IR89]. One-way permutations trivially imply one-way functions as every one-way permutation is a one-way function. It remains open whether one-way permutations can be constructed from one-way functions. The above result that one-way permutations cannot be shown *NP*-complete under commonly held assumptions while one-way functions exist that can be shown *NP*-complete would tend to suggest that no such black-box construction exists.

Akavia et al. show that if a one-way function is *NP*-hard to invert in the average case, then co*NP* $\subseteq$ *A.M.* [AGGM06]. It is generally believed that co*NP* is not a subset of *A.M.* so this is an even stronger result suggesting that it is not possible to construct a one-way function that is *NP*-hard to invert in the average case. This result was built on results by Feigenbaum and Fortnow [FF93], and Bogdanov and Trevisan [BT03]. Our system is weaker than a one-way function.

Although we cannot build a one-way function that is NP-hard on average to invert, Ajtai has discovered a relationship between average-case complexity and worst-case complexity for lattice problems that can be used to build cryptographic primitives which are secure if the *LLL* algorithm is optimal or nearly optimal [Ajt04, Mic07]. This suggests that our approach to complexity-based cryptography can be made to succeed.

2.1.2   Generic Complexity

Complexity classes deal with worst-case complexity. In worst-case complexity, a problem is considered to be hard even if only a small number of its instances is hard. Another type of complexity, called average-case complexity, is also not satisfactory as a system is cryptographically strong if a significant minority of its instances are easy to break. A cryptographer wants to base a system on a problem for which breaking almost every instance is hard. This concept is captured by *generic complexity* [GMMU07]. A language $L \subseteq \Sigma^*$ is said to have generic complexity $O(f(n))$ if, for all but a negligible subset of Σ^n, L can be decided in $O(f(n))$ time for a given measure. The definition of generic complexity requires that a measure function be defined on the problem in order for negligible to be defined. There are different definitions of negligible depending on how strongly generic a function is, but generally it is based on taking the limit as the measure goes to infinity. The usefulness of a generic complexity result depends on how well-chosen the measure is.

Many problems that are hard in the worst-case and even some that are undecidable have generically polynomial time algorithms relative to some natural measure. This means that it is not enough for cryptographic security to prove the complexity of breaking a system in the worst-case, security based on complexity must also be shown to be hard generically, or at least not be generically polynomial time, in order for the security to be derived from the complexity class. Since it is not known how to prove a cryptosystem secure if problems in a complexity class are difficult, this additional requirement makes it even more unlikely that a cipher will be proven difficult to break.

An example of a one-way function which is *NP*-complete to invert, but is generically easy to invert, is the function used by Kozen [Koz06]. This function takes a Boolean formula and a set of assignments as inputs then outputs the Boolean formula and the result of the evaluation of the formula using the assignments as outputs. This function is *NP*-complete to invert because it is possible to convert any instance of SAT to a value in the range of the function and then read a witness from the input. However, on all but a negligible number of outputs, finding an input that makes the output true is easy [GMMU07].

2.2   The Quantum Adversary

Shor showed in 1994 that quantum algorithms can factor and compute discrete logarithms efficiently [Sho94], and this was followed by other quantum algorithmic advances. To date, no efficient quantum algorithms are publicly known to exist for 3SAT or any other *NP*-complete problem. Still, the power of quantum algorithms to improve over the efficiency of conventional computers for problems believed to be computationally intractable was quite surprising, and has led some people to wonder if quantum algorithms can compute *every* computable function efficiently.

While it is not yet known whether efficient quantum algorithms exist for *NP*-complete problems, there are known limits on quantum algorithms that imply that there are no efficient "black-box" algorithms for *NP*-complete problems. Specifically, Bennett et al. [BBBV97] showed a lower bound for a problem known as Grover's Search Problem [Gro96]. They also showed a related lower bound showing that $\Omega(2^{n/2})$ oracle queries are required for the class *NP* relative to an oracle chosen uniformly at random. Furthermore, $\Omega(2^{n/3})$ oracle queries are required for *NP* ∩ co*NP*. This is the class where all one-way permutations exist [Bra79].

("Oracles" essentially allow an algorithm to freely access the results of a particular function without being charged for the computation time [Koz06]. We define this more formally in Chapter 3.) We briefly overview Grover's Search Problem here. Grover's Search Problem is defined as follows. Consider a function
$f : \{0,1\}^n \rightarrow \{0,1\}$. The problem is to find x such that $f(x) = 1$ (or, in the decision version of the problem, to determine if there is such an x—i.e, a witness). The
actual computation of f is viewed as an oracle and the complexity is the number
of times the function is evaluated.[1] Grover's Search Algorithm [Gro96] is quadratically better than a classical exhaustive search algorithm (that would try every x)
on Grover's Search Problem.

It may seem like magic that Grover's Search Algorithm can find a witness using
$O(2^{n/2})$ queries to the oracle. Here is a brief explanation of how this is done. A
quantum bit or *qubit* is composed of two complex *amplitudes* which form a unit
vector. This is written $\alpha|0\rangle + \beta|1\rangle$, where $\alpha, \beta \in \mathbb{C}$, and $|\alpha|^2 + |\beta|^2 = 1$. The
qubit can only be *measured* as a 1 or a 0. The probability of measuring a qubit
$\alpha|0\rangle + \beta|1\rangle$ as a 0 is $|\alpha|^2$ and the probability of measuring it as a 1 is $|\beta|^2$. A qubit
can be represented as a unit vector in three-dimensional space. The area that the
vector can occupy represents a sphere with radius 1. The Y-axis represents α and
the X-axis represents β. The Z-axis represents the imaginary component of the
amplitudes. It is often simplified by showing it as a circle. Quantum operations
represent a manipulation of the vector such as reflection or rotation.

In Grover's Search Algorithm, the Y-axis represents the correct answer while
the X-axis represents an incorrect answer. (See Figure 1 on page 12). The vector
starts at θ above the X-axis and rotates by 2θ with each query of the oracle. The
resulting angle is $(2m + 1)\theta$ where m is the number of queries. The probability

---

[1]This technique can also be used to construct an oracle for which $P \neq NP$ [BGS75, Koz06].

of getting the correct answer is then $\sin^2((2m+1)\theta)$. θ is approximately $\frac{1}{2^n}$ so $m = O(2^{n/2})$ in order for $\sin^2((2m+1)\theta)$ to be 1.

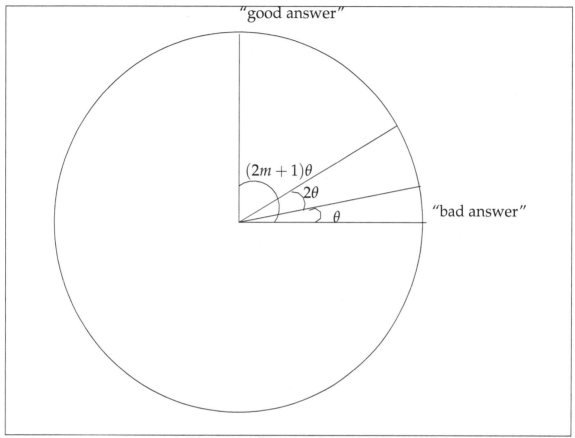

Figure 1: Grover's Algorithm

In order to make this work, some simple quantum operations are done that rotate the quantum state by 2θ. These operations are simple applications of modern technology. The challenge in implementing this is to make a system with many qubits. Some physicists predict that this will be possible in fifteen to twenty-five years [E0506, Jud07, Ahl06].

Bennett et al. [BBBV97] show that the algorithm proposed by Grover, which is quadratically better than classical brute-force search, is provably optimal for Grover's Search Problem. As mentioned above, they show that any quantum algorithm for Grover's Search Problem requires $\Omega(2^{n/2})$ queries to f. This already shows that there are some limits on the efficiency achievable by quantum computers. Furthermore, they also show a specific hardness result related to *NP*. Specifically, they show in the worst case, that relative to a particular oracle, quantum algorithms for *NP* problems must make at least $\Omega(2^{n/2})$ oracle queries. Although this does not directly address whether efficient quantum algorithms exist for *NP*-complete problems, it does imply that there is no efficient "black-box" method to solve *NP*-complete problems for this model of quantum computation in polynomial time.

2.3   Proposed Post-Quantum Systems

In this section, we survey existing post-quantum cryptosystems. We also consider key-exchange systems based on physical properties.

Attempts at basing cryptosystems on *NP*-complete problems started as early as 1978 with a cipher proposed by Merkle and Hellman [Odl90, MH78]. The goal was to create a system such that breaking it would result in the solution to a *NP*-hard problem. This was in the early days of both complexity theory and public-key cryptography, so what this would mean was not yet understood. The knapsack problem is the problem of selecting a set of weights out of a given set that add up to a given value. It can be formulated either as an optimization problem or a decision problem.

Knapsack cryptosystems operate by encoding the message as a superincreasing knapsack problem. The weights are multiplied by a constant modulus which is an integer larger than the largest weight. The ciphertext is a permutation of these modified weights. This is known as the *singly-iterated Merkle-Hellman cryptosystem*. A multiply-iterated version of it was also tried [Odl90]. The singly-iterated variant was broken by Shamir in 1982 [Sha84]. The multiply-iterated variant was broken in 1984 by Brickell [Bri84, BO88]. Another knapsack system, based on finite fields, was proposed by Chor and Rivest in 1984 [CR84], and was not broken until 2001 [Vau01]. In the end, if $NP \neq coNP$, as is generally believed, efforts to make a public-key cryptosystem that is NP-hard to break are doomed due to Brassard's theorem and similar results [Bra79, AGGM06]. In each of the knapsack cryptosystems, a restriction of the knapsack problem to the superincreasing knapsack problem (which is easy) has proved its undoing. While it may be possible to design a strong cipher based on the knapsack problem, such a cipher could not be NP-complete unless $NP = coNP$.

Another approach that has been taken to attempting to make post-quantum ciphers has been to use braid groups [KLC^{+}00]. There are a number of problems associated with braid groups that appear to be intractable. The GENERALIZED CONJUGACY SEARCH PROBLEM and the CONJUGACY DECOMPOSITION PROBLEM were used in the system by Ko et al. The first problem is used to make one-way functions and the second is used to make a key-agreement scheme. These problems are also used to make a public-key cryptosystem. Myasnikov et al. [MSU06] observed that it may not be necessary to be able to compute every instance of these problems to break the system, just a significant number that are used for the cryptosystem. This is based on generic complexity that measures the difficulty of all instances of a problem except for a negligible set [GMMU07]. They developed an approach that solved almost all instances and thus broke the cryptosystems based on braid groups.

NTRU, a novel public-key scheme using polynomial algebra, was first introduced at the rump session of Crypto '96 but was not published until 1998 [HPS98]. By this time, Coppersmith and Shamir had devised a method for breaking it using lattice-basis reduction [CS97]. However, Silverman suggested that this attack was not efficient enough to break NTRU with appropriately chosen parameters [Sil99]. A signature scheme based on NTRU was also developed [HPS01]. Many more attacks on NTRU and its improvements were devised and the status of the system is currently uncertain [EJJ00, GS02, Gen01, HGNP$^+$03, HG07].

The use of Hidden Field Equations (HFE) for cryptography was first proposed by Patarin in 1996 [Pat96]. Many instances of HFE were found to be easy in 1999 [KS99] and further cryptanalytic work continued in the early 2000's [Cou01, FJ03]. In 2005, Ding and Schmidt applied internal perturbation to HFE cryptosystems. A new perturbed variant was introduced in 2007 by Ding et al. [DGS07]. Hidden Field Equations are based on the *NP*-complete QUADRATIC CONGRUENCES problem. The Matsumoto-Imai cryptosystem uses a hidden field and a vector space to produce a public-key cryptosystem [MI83]. It was broken by Patarin using linearization in 1995. Ding proposed a perturbed version of the Matsumoto-Imai system in 2004 [Din04]. Fouque et al. broke this with a differential attack in 2005 [FGS05, DGS07]. Another type of hidden field equation scheme is oil-vinegar. Oil-Vinegar schemes are used to construct digital signatures. Oil-Vinegar schemes are based on multivariate quadratic equations with two groups of variables, the "oil" variables and the "vinegar" variables. There are three classes of these schemes, balanced, unbalanced, and Rainbow [MI83, Pat97, KPG99, DS05, DGS07]. The balanced and unbalanced schemes contain security risks [DGS07]. The Rainbow scheme may be secure [DS05, DGS07].

In 1997, Goldreich et al. proposed a one-way trapdoor function based on the CLOSEST VECTOR PROBLEM (CVP) in lattice reduction [GGH97]. From this function they obtained public-key ciphers and digital signatures. The public-key and the private-key are bases of a lattice. The public key is chosen to allow efficient one-way computation of the lattice while the private key is chosen to allow efficient approximation of the CVP. Micciancio improved the efficiency of this system in 2001 [Mic01]. A different improvement was suggested by Paeng et al. in 2003 [PJH03]. Another lattice-based system was proposed by Ajtai and Dwork in 1997 [AD97]. Collision-free hash functions based on lattice-based cryptography were proposed by Micciancio and Regev in 2004 and by Regev in 2006 [MR04, Reg06]. Regev introduced Fourier analysis in lattice-based construction in 2004, producing a new public-key cryptosystem which is a major improvement on the one by Atjai and Dwork [Reg04]. In 2006 Nguyen and Regev discovered a cryptanalytic technique on digital signature schemes including the one by Goldreich et al., and one based on NTRU [NR06]. In 2008, Pujo and Stehlé developed results on the numerical stability of the floating-point vector enumeration algorithm [PS08]. This will enable future results on the efficiency of floating-point algorithms.

A radical improvement in the speed of lattice-basis reduction by Backes and Wetzel promises improved cryptanalytic results in the future [BW07]. A better analysis of the Kannan's Shortest Lattice Vector Algorithm by Hanrot and Stehlè yields new information on what key sizes should be used in lattice-based systems [GS07]. Experiments have also been done to determine the average efficiency of lattice reduction techniques [GN08]. New attacks combining lattice reduction and meet-in-the middle by Howsgrave-Graham show promise against NTRU and may eventually be useful against other lattice-based systems [HG07].

Although first proposed before 1970 by Wiesner [BB84b], quantum key-distribution did not appear in the literature until 1983 [Wie83]. This was quickly followed by the BB84 quantum key exchange system [BB84a], which has been shown to be secure if certain well-established theories in physics hold [SP00]. Another scheme has been proposed based on thermal noise that does not make use of quantum-mechanical properties [MGK06].

Esponda et al. proposed the use of SAT to encode databases in a negative form [EAFH04, EFH04a, EFH04b, Esp05]. The algorithm is deterministic and the resulting SAT instance may be exponentially long on the input. Esponda et al. did not make any security claims about this system, but we include it here because if it is secure against classical algorithms, then there are no known efficient quantum attacks.

Our secure set-membership system also is based on SAT, specifically 3SAT. We make a security assumption about overconstrained problems and claim that our system is difficult to break if this assumption is true. We use our system to solve the secure set membership problem. This is a less-complex problem than one-way functions, but is also a natural problem that arises in cryptographic protocols.

2.4 Ciphers

In this section, we look at the existing ciphers that we considered in our designs for the Pineapple cipher and the Dragonfire cipher described in Chapter 4. We include both ciphers that have been broken and ones that have not for a careful look at the technology of block ciphers.

The strongest of the ciphers that we considered were designed for the AES competition which specified key lengths of 128, 192, and 256 bits. Although Grover's algorithm [Gro96] only gives a quadratic advantage, Bennett et al. show an upper bound for efficiency gain of f^3 over classical exhaustive search for the intersection of NP and $coNP$ using black-box methods [BBBV97]. The post-quantum model requires key lengths of at least 384 bits as key lengths must be multiplied by at least three to head off the potential cubic advantage of quantum computers. This is still the tightest known bound. One thing that all the ciphers we discuss except for Blowfish have in common is that they do not have keys long enough for the post-quantum model. Rijndael can be used with longer key sizes, but that is not supported under the Advanced Encryption Standard [DR99]. That means that each of them would have to be iterated with different keys to use for our purposes.

Most symmetric-key ciphers are based on the Feistel design, where the data block is repeatedly broken into two halves, an operation is done on one of the halves using the other half and a value known as a subkey, and the halves are then swapped (see Figure 4) [SM88, MvOV97]. In the Feistel design, values known as subkeys are derived from the key. The process of creating subkeys from keys is known as *key scheduling*. The early ciphers, such as FEAL and DES are refinements on the Feistel design [dB88, Nat99] while later ciphers such as Rijndael vary more from the classic Feistel design [DR99]. Pineapple and Dragonfire are based on the Feistel design, although our new techniques can be used with variants on Feistel. SAFER introduces field operations for the S-boxes as well as the use of exponentiation modulo a Fermat prime [Mas94]. Both Pineapple and Dragonfire use this technique. GOST introduces S-boxes as a cryptovariable [GOS89], while Blowfish introduces keyed S-boxes [Sch93]. Twofish is a refinement of Blowfish which also has an advanced key-scheduling algorithm [SKW+98]. AES expands the idea of using a field for the S-boxes and also departs significantly from the Feistel design [DR99]. Figure 2 shows how these ciphers relate and each cipher is discussed in detail below.

FEAL stands for Fast Encryption Algorithm. FEAL was intended to be implemented in software on small microcomputers such as the IBM PC XT [SM88]. New cryptanalytic techniques are often tried first on FEAL. FEAL was the first target of differential cryptanalysis and linear cryptanalysis in the open literature

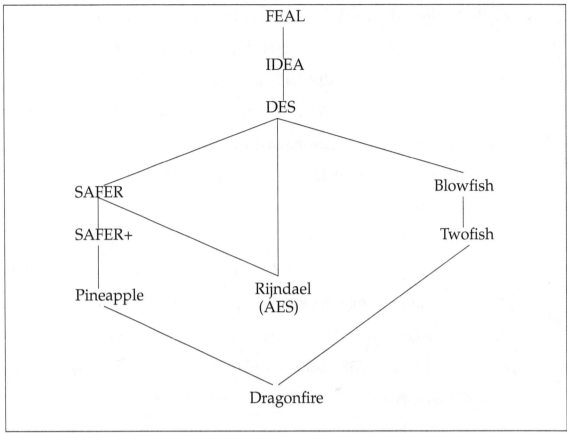

Figure 2: Evolution of Block Ciphers

[Sch96, dB88].

FEAL is an example of a Feistel cipher. FEAL was originally proposed with four rounds. That was broken. It was then proposed with eight rounds. That too was broken. It was then proposed with sixteen rounds. That was broken. FEAL-N was then proposed with an arbitrary number of rounds [Sch96].

FEAL is complete, meaning that every output bit depends on every input bit (see Section 3.1 on page 25), after four rounds. Furthermore FEAL shows the avalanche effect, meaning that changing a single input bit causes, on average, half of the output bits to change (see Section 3.1) after four rounds [Fum88].

IDEA has a block size of 64 bits and a key size of 128 bits and is intended for either hardware or software implementation [LM91b].

The IDEA cipher is based on doing three different group operations on 16-bit blocks. The group operations are bitwise exclusive or, modular addition, and modular multiplication. Since the modulus for the addition and multiplication are different, the groups satisfy the properties that no pair of operations satisfies a distributive law and no pair of operations satisfies an associative law. IDEA is based on the design principles of *confusion* which states that the function should be complicated and *diffusion* which is the principle that every bit of plaintext or key should influence every output bit [LM91b]. Confusion and diffusion were first identified as goals to pursue in ciphers by Shannon in 1949 [Sha49].

A difficulty with IDEA is that all the group operations used are linear, which violates the design principle that S-boxes should be nonlinear. That being said, IDEA appears to be a fairly strong cipher based on the results of cryptanalytic attacks [Sch96].

DES, which is an acronym for the Data Encryption Standard, is the classic example of a Feistel cipher. Machines have been designed and presented at cryptology conferences that can break it quickly using exhaustive search, [Way93], and one was built in 1998 that succeeded in breaking DES [Gil98]. Although it is now obsolete, DES's design can be instructive. A variant of it known as triple-DES, which applies DES three times with either two or three keys, is still regarded as a useful and strong cipher [MvOV97].

The Data Encryption Standard was introduced in the mid nineteen seventies [Nat99]. It is an example of a Feistel cipher. See Figure 4 on page 39 [MvOV97].

DES has sixteen rounds. The subkeys are scheduled from a single 56-bit key using a bit selection function. The block size is 64 bits and the S-boxes are 6-bits wide in the input and 4-bits wide in the output. There is no net loss of data because the data is expanded before the S-box substitution is done [Nat99].

GOST 28147-89 was adopted in 1989 by the Soviet Union for the encryption of data. The classification level of data it was intended for is not clear. GOST operates on 64-bit blocks of data with a 256-bit key. GOST operates in 32 rounds [GOS89]. GOST has several interesting features. The most important is that GOST does not define the S-boxes. The S-boxes are specific to the network being protected and are to be kept secret. GOST is a Feistel cipher (see Figure 4 on page 39). It uses a combination of modulo 2^{32} addition and XOR where most ciphers would normally use an XOR. The round permutation function for GOST is a left circular shift [GOS89]. The GOST standard stated that it was for official use and that all government agencies in the U.S.S.R. that use cryptography were obligated to use it [GOS89].

Rijndael is also known as the Advanced Encryption Standard (AES). It was selected for standardization in an open, 3-year competition. AES has a number of features including key expansion, key scheduling, and round transformation. We focus on the round transformation. The round transformation has four components: ByteSub, ShiftRow, MixColumn, and AddRoundKey. The interesting, which is to say nonlinear, part of the round transformation is ByteSub. This serves the function of an S-box substitution in a Feistel cipher and may also be implemented as a lookup table. The ByteSub table for AES is the result of polynomial multiplication using $GF(2^8)$ [DR99].

Using an algebraic group for this transformation has made it possible for Murphy and Robshaw to find a large, sparse, overdetermined set of quadratic equations which describe AES. If solved, these equations will break AES [MR02]. Solving this system is not believed to be easy as the language of solving a quadratic equation modulus an integer, called QUADRATIC CONGRUENCES, is known to be *NP*-complete [GJ79].

Blowfish is a Feistel cipher with a 64-bit block size and a variable key size of up to 448 bits. Blowfish uses four different eight-bit S-boxes to work on the different bytes of the half-word. Blowfish proceeds in sixteen rounds. The key scheduling algorithm for Blowfish is noteworthy. Blowfish generates 4168 bits of subkey from the key by feeding the key through an algorithm which initializes the S-boxes. Key-dependent S-boxes are a key feature of Blowfish. This initialization is somewhat computation-intensive, but after that, the encryption is fast and can be performed on small systems [Sch93]. Like Blowfish, Dragonfire uses keyed S-boxes.

Twofish is a Feistel-like cipher that was designed for the AES competition. It is a cipher with keyed S-boxes as well as conventional subkeys. In this respect Dragonfire is similar to it. Twofish expands its keys into the S-boxes (which are not necessarily balanced–i.e. the number of times an output symbol is produced is not uniform over the input symbols) and the subkeys. The S-boxes are determined using matrix multiplication while the subkeys are determined with a short sum of bits from the actual key [SKW+98]. The key scheduling algorithm may give the cipher a property which we call *pseudo-independence* which means that learning the bits of one subkey does not easily lead to bits of another subkey (see Definition 1 on page 66). Dragonfire has an advanced key-scheduling algorithm providing pseudo-independence.

SAFER+ was a candidate for the Advanced Encryption Standard developed by Massey, Khachatrian, and Kuregian based on the SAFER cipher [Cor98, Mas94]. SAFER operates only on bytes, which makes it very fast. SAFER uses exponentiation and logarithm of a single generator for non-linearity. This makes Pineapple similar to it. Dragonfire also uses exponentiation modulo a Fermat prime. It is different in that it uses the same generator for each S-box. Security research showing that SAFER is resistant to cryptanalysis applies to Pineapple and Dragonfire (see

Section 4.5 on page 58). Additionally, Pineapple may be stronger because of the heterogeneous S-boxes and Dragonfire may be stronger than Pineapple due to the keyed S-boxes.

To summarize Dragonfire's use of existing concepts, Dragonfire is a Feistel cipher, uses exponentiation modulo a Fermat prime like SAFER, has keyed S-boxes like Blowfish and Twofish, and has advanced key scheduling like Twofish. Two new techniques are present in the Dragonfire design: polymorphic S-boxes and pseudo-independent subkeys. These are discussed in Chapter 4.

Chapter 3

Definitions and Models of

Computation

This chapter contains many of the definitions used in this thesis including definitions related to the models of computation used to determine complexity or expected complexity. The definitions in this chapter which are defined in other works are sufficiently detailed for this thesis; where more detailed definitions exist, they may be obtained from the cited sources.

3.1 Block Ciphers

A *symmetric-key cipher* is a pair of efficiently computable functions: $e : x \times k \to y$ and $d : y \times k \to x$ where x is called the plaintext, y is called the ciphertext, and k is called the key. It should be difficult to learn x from y without the key, k. The *keysize* is $|k|$. A block cipher is a symmetric-key cipher where $|x| = |y| > 1$ is fixed. The length $|x|$ is called the *block size* [Sti02].

A system is called an *iterated block cipher* or simply an *iterated cipher* if it is a block cipher in which a simple function is repeatedly applied on the intermediate value or part of the intermediate value in a series of rounds. A *subkey* derived from the key may be applied in each round. Parameters to an iterated cipher include the number of rounds, the block size, and the size of the key. An iterated cipher with subkeys must also have a *key scheduling algorithm* to derive the subkeys from the key [MvOV97].

An iterated cipher with a block size of $2t$ is called a Feistel cipher if the input data is broken into two t-bit blocks at each round i, these blocks are called R_i, L_i; and in the round function, a function f is specified such that $L_i = R_{i-1}$ and $R_i = L_{i-1} \oplus f(R_{i-1}, K_i)$ where K_i is the subkey for the ith round [MvOV97]. Typically the function, f, is composed of three parts. In the first part, R_{i-1} is combined with the subkey, K_i. In the second part, small words of the result of the first part are used as an index into a substitution table, called an *S-box*, and the words of the result of the second part is the value found in the S-box. In the third part the result of the second part is permuted with a *permutation function*. This means that the bits are not changed but their positions are according to a fixed permutation. It is the permutation function that allows the results of the different S-boxes to be combined.

If the permutation function makes input bits of several S-boxes dependent on the output bits of a given S-box in the previous round, we say that the the permutation function *diffuses* the output of this S-box into the inputs of the affected S-boxes in the next round. If an S-box makes an output bit dependent on several input bits, we say that it *confuses* the input bits.

A cipher is *complete* if every output bit logically depends on every input bit. [MvOV97]. The *avalanche effect* occurs when a change of any single input bit causes each of the output bits to change with probability $1/2$ [Fum88, MvOV97].

A *cryptovariable* is a value in a cryptosystem, such as a key, that is kept secret. A cryptovariable is said to be *compromised* if the adversary learns it.

An S-box is *balanced* if each output symbol occurs an equal number of times when all the input symbols are tried [YT95].

3.2 Turing Machines

A *deterministic Turing machine* is a model of computation described in texts such as [HMU01, Pap95, Koz06, DSW94] and consists of an alphabet Σ, a tape, a set of states, a transition function, and a tape alphabet which includes a space symbol. The transition function shows how to change configurations by taking a symbol (under the tape read/write head) and a state to return a new symbol (to be written), a new state, and a direction to move the read/write head. A *nondeterministic Turing machine* is like a deterministic Turing machine except that there is a transition relation rather than a function. A deterministic Turing machine is in a single configuration at any given time while a nondeterministic Turing machine may be in multiple configurations simultaneously. These multiple configurations can alternatively be described as choosing from among multiple successor states and always choosing correctly. Starting from a configuration of a nondeterministic Turing machine and selecting only one subsequent configuration from the possible subsequent configurations from the transition relation, and continuing to do this recursively, yields a *path of computation*. A deterministic Turing Machine is said to *accept* its input if it halts in an accepting state while a nondeterministic Turing Machine is said to accept its input if at least one path of computation halts in an accepting state. Likewise a deterministic Turing machine rejects its input if it halts in a rejecting state while a nondeterministic Turing Machine rejects its input if all paths of computation halt in a rejecting state.

Alternating Turing machines may be found in texts such as [Koz06]. An *alternating Turing machine* uses a relation rather than a function for the transition function like a nondeterministic Turing machine. This results in a tree of configurations for an input. States in an alternating Turing machine may be labeled with a $\neg$, a $\vee$ or a $\wedge$ so that configurations may alternate between the closest higher configuration on the tree being a $\vee$ and a $\wedge$. A $\neg$ label indicates that the value of children should be reversed. There may be a finite number of alternations. A $\wedge$ means that all computation paths descending from the current configuration must accept for the path to accept and a $\vee$ means that at least one computation path descending from the current configuration must accept in order for the path to accept.

A *probabilistic Turing machine* is a Turing machine with an additional tape of random bits which may be read sequentially and not written [Koz06]. The resulting computation may be a function of the random bits as well as the input. If two probabilistic Turing machines have the same random bits, same states, and same transition function we call them *random clones*.

An *oracle Turing machine* as defined in [Koz06] is a Turing machine with an oracle tape. The oracle Turing machine may write strings to the oracle tape and enter a special state where the oracle replies by writing a single symbol to the oracle tape which may be read.

A *language* $L \subseteq \Sigma^*$ is a (possibly infinite) set of strings written with the alphabet Σ. A *class* is a (possibly infinite) set of languages [HMU01, DSW94]]. A language $L \subseteq \Sigma^*$ *is decided* by a Turing machine, M, if for any $x \in L$ as input, M halts in an accepting state and for any $x' \notin L$, M halts in a rejecting state [HMU01, DSW94]. Turing machine A *simulates* a Turing machine B if A produces the same output as B [Lyn96].

3.3   Complexity Classes

Information on complexity (including *NP*-completeness) is available in Garey
and Johnson's 1979 book [GJ79] as well as more modern texts[1] [Pap95, Koz06,
Koz92].

A *complexity class* is a class whose membership is determined by the existence of
a Turing machine with some specified property or resource bound that can decide
the language.

Given a language $L \subseteq \Sigma^*$ and a set of valid instances: $U \subseteq \Sigma^*$, the complement
of L is $\overline{L} \subseteq U$ such that:

$$x \in L \Leftrightarrow x \notin \overline{L}$$

Given a class C, $\mathrm{co}C$ is the set of languages which are complements of languages
in C [Koz06].

A function $f : \mathbb{N} \mapsto \mathbb{N}$ is said to be *polynomially bounded* if there exist $k, c \in \mathbb{N}$
such that $n > c \Rightarrow f(n) < n^k$ [Koz06].   The complexity classes P and NP
can be found in many texts [GJ79, Pap95, Koz06]. The complexity class P is the
class of languages which can be decided by a deterministic Turing machine in a
polynomially-bounded number of configurations. The complexity class NP is the
class of languages which can be decided by a nondeterministic Turing machine
with each computation path having a polynomially-bounded number of configurations.

The complexity class Σ_k^P is the class of languages which can be decided by an
alternating Turing machine starting with a $\vee$ and having at most k alternations.
Similarly, Π_k^P is the class of languages that can be decided by an alternating Turing

---

[1][GJ79] contains reductions for many *NP*-complete problems. [Pap95] focuses on *NP*. [Koz06]
discusses many complexity classes and prerequisites may be found in [Koz92], a quarter of which
is about complexity classes.

Machine starting with a $\wedge$ and having at most k alternations. $NP = \Sigma_1^P$ and $coNP = \Pi_1^P$. The *polynomial hierarchy, PH,* is the class of languages which are accepted by Σ_k^P or Π_k^P for some k [Koz06]. *PSPACE* is the class of languages which can be decided by a Turing Machine using a polynomially-bounded on the size of the input amount of space on its tape [Koz06].

Logspace and polynomial reducibility are defined in many texts [GJ79, Pap95, Koz06]. Given a language $A \subseteq \Sigma^*$ and a language $B \subseteq \Delta^*$, we say that A is logspace reducible to B, denoted $A \leq_M^{\log} B$, if there exists a function $\sigma : \Sigma^* \mapsto \Delta^*$ which can be computed by a deterministic Turing machine using $\lceil \log_2 n + 1 \rceil$ space for n input symbols. Similarly we say that A is polynomially-reducible to B and write $A \leq_M^P B$ if σ can be computed in a polynomially-bounded number of configurations on a deterministic Turing machine.

The idea of completeness is discussed in many standard texts [GJ79, Pap95, Koz92, Koz06]. We say that a language L is *complete* for a complexity class C, denoted C-complete, if $X \in C \Leftrightarrow X \leq_M^{\log} L$ and $L \in C$. If every language in C is reducible to L (but L may not be in C) then L is said to be C-hard. Likewise we say that a language L is *polynomially complete* for a complexity class C if $L \in C$ and $X \in C \Leftrightarrow X \leq_M^P L$. Note that all languages that are C-complete are C-hard.

The *counting problem* on a language is the integer valued function that takes an instance and returns the number of witnesses that make it true. For any integer valued function whose range can be bounded by a function $g : \Sigma^* \mapsto \mathbb{N}$, computable in a polynomially-bounded number of configurations, $f : \Sigma^* \mapsto \mathbb{N}$, there is an oracle $\geq_f$ that takes as its input $x\#t$ and writes "yes" if $f(x) \geq t$ or "no" if $f(x) < t$. Using binary search [Knu98, AHU74, CLRS01], a Turing Machine with the oracle $\geq_f$ can output the value $f(x)$ in $\lceil \log_2 g(x) + 1 \rceil$ oracle queries. The complexity class *#P* is the class of languages decidable in a polynomially-bounded number of configurations of a deterministic Turing Machine relative to an oracle $\geq_{\#L}$ where $\#L$ is the number of witnesses for an instance of $L \in NP$ [Koz06]. For example, the counting problem on SAT is the number of truth assignments that satisfy the Boolean expression. The complexity class $A.M.$ is the class of all problems which have two-round interactive proof systems [AGGM06].

3.4   Oracle Notation

We define the class C^O of languages to be the set of languages that are in the class C using Turing machines with access to an oracle O. We call this C *relative to* O. If O is a language, then we are considering an oracle that decides that language; if it is a class of languages, then it is an oracle that decides every language in the class, i.e., a language complete for the class [Koz06, DSW94].

3.5   Zero Knowledge

A protocol for proving a proposition is *zero knowledge* if the verifier, with no more information than the proposition to be demonstrated, can produce transcripts identical to those which are produced by the interaction between the prover and the verifier [MvOV97].

Chapter 4

Dragonfire: A Cipher With Polymorphic S-boxes

The systems proposed in Chapter 5 require random or pseudorandom number generators. Toward the goal of constructing a new pseudorandom number generator for use in this thesis, as well as for the purpose of developing a new post-quantum cipher, we develop a symmetric-key cryptosystem[1] and show how it can be adapted to make a pseudorandom number generator. This cipher includes two novel techniques called *polymorphic S-boxes* and *pseudo-independent subkeys*. These techniques can be used to make many new ciphers; ours is just an example.

Symmetric-key ciphers are post-quantum because, although they are $O(1)$ to break, the constants for known cryptanalytic techniques are large enough to make them infeasible to break (these constants are called the *work factors*). Quantum computers can not get more than a cubic advantage using black box methods if the cipher is secure against attacks other than exhaustive search [BBBV97].

There are many ciphers and associated pseudorandom number generators, as

---

[1]Patent pending, [dM08].

well as other methods of generating pseudorandom bits. Symmetric-key cryptography is not a solved problem as revealed in the United States's accusation that an Iraqi revealed to the Iranians that the United States broke their cipher [RJ04, Coc07]. There is no reason to think that the Iranians are incompetent at cryptography. Iran is the dominant regional military power in the Middle East with a gross GDP in 2006, the latest year for which information is available, of more than $599 billion dollars. The Iranian government ran a budget surplus in 2006 with revenues of more than $110 billion. Iranian military expenditures in 2006 were 2.5 percent of GDP or about $15 billion [Age07]. The Iranians have access to the same open literature as Western civilian cryptographers, including the designers of AES. Based on this, it is natural to conclude that the U.S. government has cryptanalytic techniques which can break many popular ciphers. Based on the fact that the Iranian cipher was broken and reasons to believe that the Iranians have a sufficient investment in cryptography, it is natural to conclude that the United States has powerful cryptanalytic techniques and that civilian cryptographers do not have access to these cryptanalytic techniques. It is therefore a good idea to develop new techniques in cipher design.

Unlike many other block ciphers, our cipher has a large enough key size for the post-quantum model with a single application of the cipher. This is not as important as polymorphic S-boxes and pseudo-inidependent subkeys because ciphers can be iterated with different keys to get a longer effective key length [Nat99].

Truly random bits can be quickly generated using quantum methods by sending a zero qubit through a Hadamard transform and measuring the resulting state. However, this requires special hardware that may not be technologically feasible and would also require the random bits to be preshared in the way we use it in Chapter 5 (Algorithm 11). With a secure pseudorandom number generator, a short initial state or seed may be shared and then as many pseudorandom bits as necessary may be synchronously generated. One of the popular types of pseudorandom number generators is based on elliptic curves, which are not secure in the post-quantum model [MOV93].

Iterated ciphers, particularly Feistel ciphers, have become the standard design methodology for symmetric key ciphers. While any single round can be broken easily, the iteration of the rounds sixteen times or more results in security that would not be achieved with a single round.

From DES to AES, iterated ciphers have been named as standards for the protection of communications and data. The fact that Skipjack is iterated and was developed by the National Security Agency, [BBD+99, Har97], shows that they are also used for the protection of classified information. While sophisticated cryptanalytic attacks have been developed, overall these ciphers have remained secure [Sch96, MvOV97, Sti02].

In this chapter, we explore common elements of iterated cipher design and cryptanalytic techniques against iterated ciphers as well as introducing our cipher. Iterated ciphers that we considered in our design are studied in Section 2.4. We also present our new proposed cipher, the Dragonfire cipher, in this chapter.

Our security analysis of Dragonfire is based on heuristic tests rather than formal proofs. The usual method of evaluating ciphers is to publish them in the literature to allow other researchers to try to develop cryptanalytic attacks on them. It is also common practice to provide a simplified version of ciphers to analyze.

Innovations in the Dragonfire cipher include balanced keyed S-boxes and pseudo-independent subkeys. Balanced keyed S-boxes have the advantages of keyed S-box ciphers such as Twofish which include making it impossible to precompute cryptanalytic tables for cryptanalytic methods such as differential cryptanalysis while also having the advantages of balanced S-boxes which are believed to have good security properties [YT95]. Pseudo-independent subkeys increase the workload of a cryptanalyst by making it difficult for him to learn bits of many subkeys by learning a bit of a single subkey.

The Dragonfire cipher is more appropriate to the post-quantum model than some other ciphers because it allows key sizes ranging from 256 bits to 1024 bits. The post-quantum model requires at least 384 bits while the AES standard only allows keys up to 256 bits. Our implementation of the Dragonfire cipher is not nearly as fast as existing implementations of AES, but some of this disparity may be related to inefficiencies in the implementation rather than inherent bottlenecks in the algorithms. Furthermore, AES would have to be iterated up to four times with different keys to obtain key lengths comparable to Dragonfire, which also reduces the disparity.

Iterated ciphers are ciphers in which a simple function is applied repeatedly. Each time the function is applied is called a round as shown in Figure 3 on page 38. In an n-round iterated cipher, the function is applied n times. The function is usually a combination of a permutation, an XOR between some or all of the intermediate text with the key, and lookups into a table called an S-box.

In this chapter, we consider the general design of iterated ciphers and cryptanalysis of iterated ciphers. Different ciphers that we considered in our design are shown in Section 2.4. Our contribution is the Dragonfire cipher and a keyed pseudo-random number generator (PRNG). We first introduce and analyze a simpler, related cipher, called Pineapple, to make assessments of the security of the system.

The methodology used in the Pineapple cipher allows us to create 2^{56} different ciphers. Dragonfire uses and extends this methodology to, in effect, allow the cipher to be selected by the key. The Dragonfire cipher takes the transparent method of generating S-boxes used by Pineapple and uses them to create a cipher with keyed S-boxes. This defeats most precomputations for cryptanalysis as the S-boxes are now different between sessions. This can also be used for keyed pseudorandom number generators (PRNGs). We construct a PRNG called the Dragonfire PRNG, which is used in other systems in this thesis (Chapter 5).

4.1 Complexity of Symmetric-Key Ciphers

As we saw in Chapter 2, one-way permutations, with some restrictions, cannot be NP-hard to invert unless $NP = \text{co}NP$ [Bra79], which is unlikely. One-way permutations are equivalent to symmetric-key ciphers because symmetric-key ciphers can be constructed from one-way permutations through stream ciphers [ILL89], and one-way permutations can be constructed from symmetric-key ciphers by fixing the key and using feedback. Therefore, it is unlikely that an NP-hard problem can be reduced to a language based on finding the plaintext of a symmetric-key cipher.

There is further evidence that no language complete in a nontrivial complexity class can be reduced to a language based on finding the plaintext of a symmetric-key cipher where the length of the key is independent of the length of the ciphertext. Suppose that such a reduction existed, then a reduction exists that encodes a language complete for that complexity class as ciphertext and gets its output as plaintext. However, since the length of the key is independent of the length of the ciphertext, the complexity of computing the plaintext is $O(1)$ relative to the size of the input using exhaustive key search. This is because any reduction will produce a ciphertext or ciphertext/plaintext pair (depending on the type of cryptanalysis) as input to the Turing machine which decides whether the key is less than a given value. The Turing machine will never need to try more than the constant number of possible keys, however, regardless of the length of the input. Thus, although the Turing machine may be very slow, it does not get slower as the ciphertext gets longer. In other words, if a problem can be reduced to a problem solved by this Turing machine, it can be solved in constant time. This means that the complexity class being reduced is trivial.

Similarly, if we were to allow the key for a symmetric-key cipher to grow polynomially in the logarithm of the size of the input, then the complexity class being reduced would be a subset of P. If the size of the key to the symmetric-key cipher were to grow linearly with the size of the input, then, based on Shannon's classic result, it would be possible to have unconditional security. There is no Turing machine that can decide or even a language that may be decided such that the Turing machine can break an unconditionally secure system or such that deciding the language would result in breaking such a system [Sha48, Sha49].

4.2 General Design

The general design of an iterated cipher is as shown in Figure 3 on page 38. What happens in the boxes marked g is of interest. In the g-function of most ciphers, part or all of the intermediate text is XORed with the subkey, a permutation is applied, and the result is broken up into words followed by some addition entangling operation. Each word is substituted by looking it up in a table known as an *S-box*. Each occurrence of g is called a round. Ciphers have many rounds.

Many iterated ciphers are Feistel schemes. In the f-function (see Figure 4), Feistel schemes divide the plaintext into halves and perform operations on one half using the key and then XOR the result with the other half [FNS75]. Figure 4 on page 39 is based on standard drawings of Feistel ciphers such as DES [MvOV97]. Examples of Feistel ciphers include DES and FEAL. Most cryptanalysis techniques for block ciphers are primarily targeted against Feistel ciphers. However, these attacks are often useful against non-Feistel ciphers such as AES.

A typical round is as in the Pineapple cipher, which is of the Feistel design (see Section 3.1). The round itself is fairly simple—and reversible with the subkey—it is the iteration of the rounds that makes the cipher hard to break. The Dragonfire cipher is also of the Feistel design.

An important construct of an iterated cipher is the S-box. The S-box, also called the *S-table*, is a lookup table whose values replace small words that are part of the block. Usually the S-boxes are *square*, meaning that the range of the values is the same as the range of the index, but some ciphers, such as DES, have S-boxes that expand or contract the words. S-boxes must be reversible in order for decryption to be possible. As we see in Section 4.3 on page 40, most attacks on iterated ciphers depend on weaknesses in the S-box. The S-box provides the non-linearity in the cipher [Sti02]. Since the S-box only deals with small words, the permutation function combines the results from different words. This is vital to the security of the cipher [Sch96].

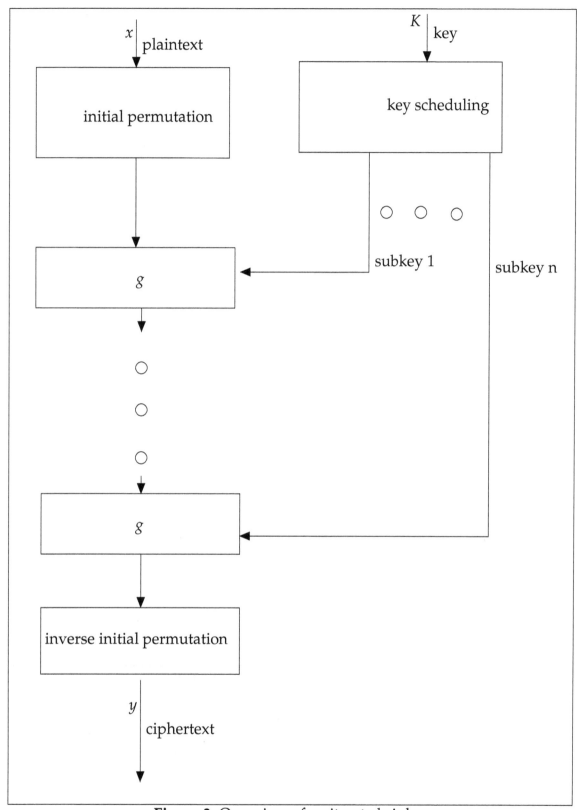

Figure 3: Overview of an iterated cipher

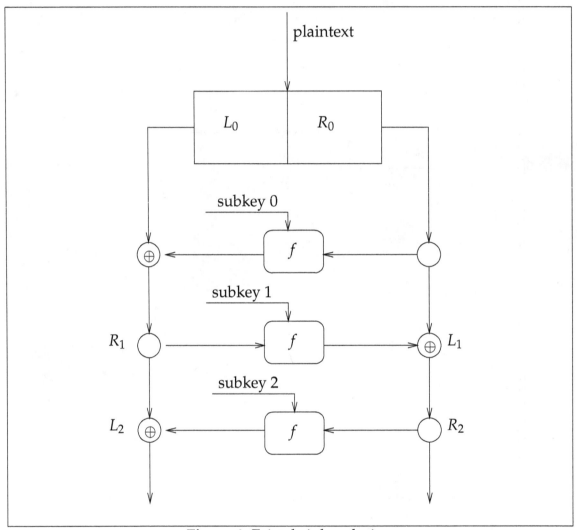

Figure 4: Feistel cipher design

4.3   Cryptanalytic Attacks

There are a number of cryptanalytic attacks on iterated ciphers that we considered when designing the Dragonfire cipher. Some are specifically for Feistel ciphers, others generalize to all iterated ciphers. Linear cryptanalysis is the most successful attack against DES. Linear cryptanalysis is a cryptanalytic attack that has shown promise against ciphers including DES and FEAL [Mat94]. Bilinear cryptanalysis is a new technique that shows great promise but has, so far, only been applied successfully to contrived ciphers [Cou04]. Differential cryptanalysis is a powerful cryptanalytic technique pioneered by Biham and Shamir [BS91b, BS91a]. Here we will briefly mention each of the attacks that we found to be relevant in designing Dragonfire.

It is important to note that we consider an attack successful if it significantly reduces the workload of a cryptanalyst even if it does not reduce the workload enough for the cryptanalyst to actually break the cipher. While DES and other ciphers that have short key sizes are actually broken with an exhaustive key search as well as with some of these attacks, these attacks do not generally reduce the work factor enough to break ciphers with key sizes of 128 or more bits.

All of the cryptanalytic techniques discussed here are known-plaintext attacks. This means that ciphertext/plaintext pairs must be known for the attacks to be carried out. In differential, linear, and bilinear cryptanalysis, so many pairs must be known that the attack is not usually practical. Algebraic cryptanalysis represents many potential types of cryptanalysis whose properties may vary.

Differential cryptanalysis has been used with great success against ciphers including DES. The idea of differential cryptanalysis is that given a pair of plaintexts, one wants to compute the probability of the difference between bits in the ciphertexts based on the difference between their plaintexts. This requires knowing many ciphertext/plaintext pairs encrypted with the same key [BS91a, LM91a]. The goal of differential cryptanalysis is to recover the encryption key.

Over the course of the early nineties, results of differential cryptanalysis of DES with increasing rounds up to the full sixteen were presented at cryptology conferences culminating in the publication of the book "The Differential Cryptanalysis of the Data Encryption Standard" by Eli Biham and Adi Shamir in 1993 with the full cryptanalysis of all rounds of DES [BS93].

Linear cryptanalysis was introduced by Matsui in 1994. It is based on the probability of a linear equation involving the plaintext, the key, and the ciphertext being satisfied [Mat94]. Linear cryptanalysis has shown success relative to exhaustive key search against a wide array of iterated ciphers [OA94, HKM95, BCQ04]. There was a great deal of interest in linear cryptanalysis in the mid-nineties and a resurgence of interest was shown in it at the Crypto 2004 cryptology conference [BCQ04].

Bilinear cryptanalysis is a relatively new technique introduced by Courtois in 2004. Bilinear cryptanalysis takes advantage of specific mathematical characteristics of Feistel ciphers. Bilinear cryptanalysis has been applied to DES, but has not been as successful as other attacks.

Like linear cryptanalysis, bilinear cryptanalysis involves a linear approximation to the cipher. Unlike linear cryptanalysis, bilinear cryptanalysis uses algebraic properties of Feistel ciphers to simplify and enhance the use of the approximations [Cou04].

Attacks have been proposed exploiting hardware faults in computation [BCS08]. These attacks exploit mistakes made during modular computation using large numbers and target public-key cryptosystems such as RSA. Block ciphers do not use this sort of computation so they are not vulnerable to these particular attacks. It is possible that an attack based on hardware faults will be developed to attack block ciphers.

In some cases a cipher can be completely modeled by a set of equations over a group. In these cases, if the set of equations can be solved, the solution yields the cipher key. As an example, AES is completely described by a set of quadratic equations [MR02]. This does not break AES because QUADRATIC CONGRUENCES is *NP*-complete [GJ79].

A new attack by Dinur and Shamir attacks systems that can be represented by low-degree polynomials [DS08]. This attack, called a cube attack, is likely to be successful on block ciphers if information is available from early in the encryption process. For a chosen-ciphertext, or chosen-plaintext attack, however, this attack is unlikely to be successful on ciphers such as Dragonfire which have large exponent exponentiation built into the S-box. Cube attacks have a complexity $O(2^{d-1})$ where d is the degree of the polynomials. As exponentiation of eight-bit values is used in each round of Dragonfire, a polynomial model of a round of Dragonfire would require high-degree polynomials.

4.4 The Pineapple Cipher

We introduce the Pineapple Cipher as a toy cipher for exploring properties of the Dragonfire cipher. We also use it as a primitive in the Dragonfire initialization algorithm. We introduce Dragonfire later in this chapter. It is useful to have a wide variety of ciphers to choose from so that if one gets broken, only a fraction of the traffic is compromised. The Pineapple Cipher is based on the well understood Feistel design.

```
Input:  k, p
Output:  c


L := p[0]..p[63];
R := p[64]..p[128];
B := k;
S[box number][index] := Pineapple S-boxes
        for i:=1 to 16 do
        begin
                L := L  XOR (B[0]..B[63]);
                ROTATE B left 16 bits;
                for j=1 to 8 do
                begin
                 L[8j+0]..L[8j+7] := S[j][L[8j+0]..L[8j+7]];
                end;
                R := L XOR R;
                SWAP L,R;
        end;
c[0]..c[63] := L;
c[64]..c[127] := R;
```

Algorithm 1: Pineapple encryption algorithm

4.4.1 Design

The defining characteristic of the Pineapple cipher is its eight S-boxes, whose construction is based on Fermat primes. Eight S-boxes are used because that is what is needed for the 64-bit half-word size. Recall that a *Fermat prime* is a prime number p, such that there exists an integer n where $p = 2^n + 1$. Examples of powers of two that are one less than Fermat primes include $n = 4$, $n = 8$ and $n = 16$ giving primes of 17, 257, and 65537. To construct the Pineapple S-boxes, we specify the Fermat prime 257—i.e., $n = 8$. This yields an 8×8 S-box, a size that is consistent with other modern ciphers. There are eight S-boxes: $j = 0, \cdots, 7$. A number, g_j, is chosen for each j such that $g_j^{2^n+1} = 1 \pmod{2^n + 1}$ but $g_j^x \neq 1 \pmod{2^n + 1}$ for $0 < x \leq 2^n$. Such a number is called a *generator*. The S-boxes are then defined as:

$$S[j][i] = g_j^i - 1 \quad (\text{mod } 2^n + 1)$$

The user may optionally add an integer constant to i in the right hand side of the equation. The SAFER cipher also uses exponentiation modulo 257 to construct S-boxes, but where SAFER uses the same generator for all of the S-boxes, Pineapple uses a different generator for each S-box.

This transparent method of choosing S-boxes prevents the introduction of trapdoors that make some types of cryptanalysis easy. Ignoring the possibility of shifting the S-box by adding a constant to the index i, 2^{56} different 128-bit ciphers with 8-bit S-boxes are possible with the same Feistel structure and permutation.

We choose 128 bits as the word size for Dragonfire for a couple of reasons. One is that 128-bit words are common in modern ciphers as a result of the AES competition. Another reason is that when operating on a half-word in the the round function, one is dealing with a perfect square. This allows our simple permutation function to work. 128-bit words do have a drawback, specifically that if the cipher is used to make a hash function or MAC, the security level will only be 64 bits due to the birthday attack [FS03]. Increasing the block size beyond 128 bits would increase the overhead for small blocks to a potentially unacceptable level.

We choose a 256-bit key to secure the cipher against conventional attacks and known quantum attacks such as Grover's algorithm [Gro96]. Relativized results for the intersection of *NP* and co*NP* suggest that a cipher should have 384 bits of key to achieve a quantum security level comparable to a 128-bit key against classical computers [BBBV97]. While this is a limitation of the Pineapple cipher, we would like to emphasize that Pineapple is a toy cipher intended to test the properties of our method of choosing S-boxes. The maximum key size for AES is also 256 bits [DR99].

S-boxes chosen in this manner are nonlinear. When using this method it is desirable to use different generators to generate different S-boxes for different sub-blocks. The Fermat primes 257 and 65537 are particularly well-suited to S-box generation because they are in the range of table sizes commonly used for S-boxes. Pineapple uses 257 to keep the table size small. Since the S-boxes are 8-bits wide, 8 of them are needed for the round function which operates on 64 bits.

Since the modulus is prime and g_j is a generator, the resulting S-box is a permutation over $\mathbb{Z}_{2^n}$. This makes it reversible and balanced.

The generators chosen to make the eight S-boxes for Pineapple are: 254 206 160 155 126 107 71 51. These generators were randomly picked from a table of generators modulo 257. This makes Pineapple S-boxes a fixed instance of Dragonfire's keyed S-boxes.

The basic design of the cipher is the Feistel design shown in Figure 4 on page 39 which is also represented in Algorithm 1 (see Section 3.1). If $x_{k,i,j}$ is the jth bit of the ith byte of the input to the kth round, then the round permutation is defined to be:

$$b_{k,j,i} = a_{k,i,j}$$

The f-function in the round is shown in Figure 5.

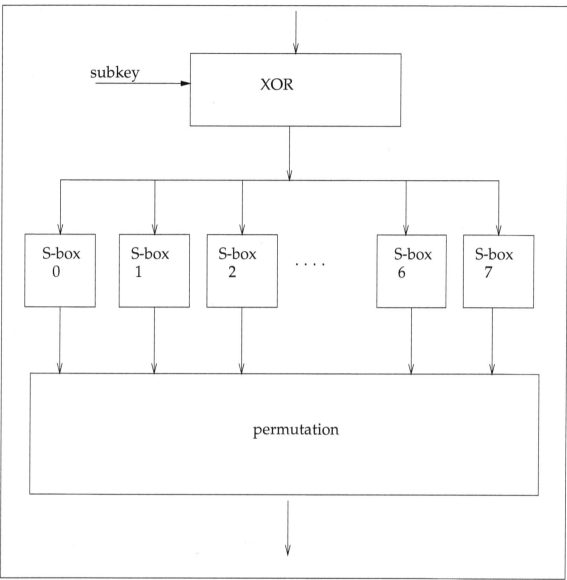

Figure 5: f-function for Pineapple and Dragonfire

Each word is 128 bits long, so the left and right halves are 64 bits each. This allows complete diffusion through the half-word in the round permutation because the half-word is the square of the S-box width. This allows the permutation function to diffuse the output of each S-box into the inputs of every other S-box in the next round. The subkey is XORed with the half-word before the S-box is applied. After the S-box is applied, the round permutation is applied.

The Pineapple cipher is theoretically complete (see Section 3.1) after three rounds because the permutation diffuses all of the subblocks in each round. This is in contrast to DES which is complete after five rounds or FEAL which is complete after four rounds [SM88]. It does not show the avalanche effect (see Section 3.1), however, until five rounds (see Table 3 on page 55).

The configuration of the Pineapple cipher is $n = 8$, a block size of 128 bits, and a key size of 256 bits. The subkeys are computed by taking the first 64 bits of the key. The key is rotated left sixteen bits after each round for encryption (right for decryption). There are sixteen rounds.

The Pineapple algorithm is described in Algorithm 1 on page 43 and Figure 4. Common Lisp programs to compute generators and S-boxes are available from the author.

4.4.2 Security

There are a number of reasons to be optimistic about the security of Pineapple. For example, random S-box permutations have proven to be strong against differential cryptanalysis [O'C95]. Since the S-box is balanced (see Section 3.1) by being a permutation and is relatively large, it is likely to be resistant to both linear and differential cryptanalysis [YT95]. The use of exponentiation in the S-box should result in highly non-linear equations for algebraic cryptanalysis. The GOST cipher [GOS89], the Blowfish cipher, [Sch93], and the Twofish cipher [SKW+98] all assume that a random S-box is likely to be cryptographically strong. If we accept this assumption, then our cipher should have a high likelihood of being strong unless the mathematical structure of our S-box has a specific property that makes it less secure. If such a property exists, it would also affect the SAFER family of ciphers. No such weakness has been discovered.

The next few paragraphs provide experimental evidence that some obvious attacks that might be tried on Pineapple will not succeed. The avalanche experiment is aimed at establishing a property of Pineapple which is needed for its use in the initialization algorithm of Dragonfire. The remaining experiments do not demonstrate that Dragonfire or Pineapple are strong, instead they merely serve as a basis for believing that there is not something inherently wrong with choosing S-boxes using exponentiation modulus a Fermat prime. Since Dragonfire does not have fixed S-boxes, these experiments would not be meaningful for it.

Data for 1,000,000,000 iterations.

input bit	output bit	number of differences	bias
29	115	500,052,745	0.000053
114	6	500,058,536	0.000059
124	0	500,061,193	0.000061
125	41	500,063,582	0.000064
43	125	500,051,715	0.000052
65	127	500,050,733	0.000051
11	10	500,051,994	0.000052
68	81	500,056,052	0.000056

Table 1: Top Disagreeing Bits for Pineapple

Correlation Experiment

In an experiment designed to test for an obvious weakness (which no cipher should have), we generate a 128x128 matrix and populate it with the number of times the corresponding two bits, one input bit and one output bit, are the same over the course of many encryptions with all of the subkeys set to zero. Zeroing out the subkeys is the same as not applying the subkeys in the cipher. If there is a statistically significant correlation, this can be used by a cryptanalyst to attack the

Data for 1,000,000,000 iterations.

input bit	output bit	number of differences	bias
24	68	499, 929, 241	0.000071
27	124	499, 935, 379	0.000065
35	120	499, 946, 841	0.000053
102	76	499, 947, 881	0.000052
25	61	499, 948, 369	0.000052
87	83	499, 939, 070	0.000061
54	123	499, 947, 685	0.000052
115	120	499, 946, 039	0.000054

Table 2: Top Agreeing Bits for Pineapple

cipher by assigning probabilities to the input bits based on the output bits. This experiment would fail if there were not a sufficient number of rounds or if the S-boxes consistently related one particular index bit to a value bit. We designed this test to check these conditions.

Sixteen of the strongest correlations were analyzed: the eight pairs that are the same the most often and the eight that are the same the least often. The algorithm for a single iteration is described in Algorithm 2 on the following page. We computed the ratio of the number of times that two bits are the same over the number of runs. The closer this ratio is to $\frac{1}{2}$ in the most extreme cases, the stronger the cipher is against some simple types of cryptanalysis which involve consulting a statistical table to learn the likely value of the keys based on a known plaintext/-ciphertext pair. In Table 1 on the previous page and Table 2 we show the results of this experiment. As the table shows, the maximum bias is approximately .00007, a value which could be caused by random noise for this number of iterations.

```
Input: int Count[128,128]
Output: int Count[128,128]
(* generate a random vector of 128 bits *)
for i=1 to 128 do
    plaintext[i]=random(2);
end;
(* encrypt it with key=0 *)
ciphertext=encrypt(plaintext, 0);
(* compare each bit of the plaintext with
   each bit of the ciphertext *)
for i=1 to 128 do
    for j=1 to 128
        if (plaintext[i] XOR ciphertext[j]) then
            Count[i,j]:=Count[i,j]+1;
```

Algorithm 2: A single iteration of the Correlation security experiment

Avalanche Experiment

The *avalanche effect* is the property that if a single input bit changes, then each output bit changes with probability $\frac{1}{2}$ [Fum88, MvOV97]. This has long been regarded as a critical property in ciphers and is required of Pineapple as it is used in the Dragonfire initialization algorithm (see Theorem 1 on page 66). To compute the actual number of rounds for the avalanche effect in Pineapple, we performed the experiment in Algorithm 3 many times and computed statistical information from the results. We found that after five rounds, the average number of changed bits was 64 which is half of the block size. This is consistent with the avalanche effect. We also kept track of the variance and calculated the standard deviation. The standard deviation becomes stable after six rounds. The results can be found in Table 3 on page 55. The experiment was run for one billion iterations on a high-performance cluster.

An iteration of this experiment chooses a random value and encrypts it with a fixed key, remembering the value after each round. A single bit in the input value is then changed. It is encrypted again, again remembering the value after each round. For each round, the two values are compared and the Hamming distance is computed and stored as the result. The avalanche effect is achieved when the value comes very close to 64. The standard deviation was also computed and we find that the avalanche effect is achieved with a stable standard deviation after 6 rounds.

Differential Cryptanalysis

We base our differential experiments on the book by Biham and Shamir [BS93]. Actual differential cryptanalysis is somewhat more complicated and requires resources and luck. We tried a simple algorithm for differential cryptanalysis on the Pineapple cipher which is described in Algorithm 4 on page 55 and operates as follows. A random key is selected for the entire experiment. For each bit, a random vector is generated and encrypted. The bit is changed and the new vector is encrypted. The difference between the two vectors is considered with each different bit counted separately. The different bits are divided by the number of iterations. The bias is calculated which is the distance between this ratio and one half. A small bias indicated that the bits look random. The eight bits that change most and least are presented in Table 4 on page 56. The number of iterations may not be sufficient to see actual statistical correlations through the noise generated by the distribution but they are enough to show that any such statistical correlations are too small to break the cipher.

The experiment was modified to try all 2-bit differences. This required 1,928 hours of runtime. It was run on Stevens Institute of Technology's HPCF cluster. The most significant differences are shown in Table 5 on page 57. The difference between the ratio of changed bits to total bits and one half is not large enough to break the cipher.

4.4.3   Performance

The Pineapple cipher was implemented in C++ using the gcc compiler and tested on an AMD Opteron 250 processor running at 2.4GHz with a 1MB cache. It encrypted 1,775.5KB per second (14,204 kbits/second)[2]. In a second test, the Pineapple cipher clocked in at 11,750 kbits/sec on a Athlon 64 X2 Dual Core Processor 4000+. Only one core was used. It was tested on a symmetric multiprocessing system, but only one CPU was used for the test. It is likely that significant performance gains could be made by coding the encryption algorithm in assembler language. The most obvious place where significant performance gains can be made is in the implementation of the permutation.

The cryptosystem fits in level 1 cache on modern processors as the S-boxes only require 2KB of memory. The code required to run the cipher fits into 3KB.

The performance bottleneck of Pineapple is in the permutation, not the S-boxes, so a much faster cipher could be built using our technique for obtaining S-boxes. We chose to use our slower permutation function because it is easier to verify that the cipher becomes complete after three rounds.

The argument works like this. If the S-boxes confuse the bits, then after the first round, each group of eight subblocks has a bit from each of the original eight subblocks. After the second round, every bit of every subblock depends on each of the original eight subblocks. After the third round, every output bit depends on every input bit.

A faster permutation may be based on shifting the bits. This would result in

---

[2]The test was run by Lincoln Decoursey using software supplied by the author.

more rounds being needed to obtain completeness and would be harder to analyze. Even using our permutation there is much room for optimization, possibly by writing the assembler code by hand with a view towards taking advantage of the superscalar aspects of the target processor.

```
Input:
Output:  Integer HammingDistance[0..16]

(* Choose a random 128 bit word, p *)
for i=1 to 128 do
begin
        p[i]:=rand(2);
end;
(* encrypt p *)
z[0]:=p;
for i:=1 to 16 do
begin
        z[i]:=round(i, z[i-1]);
        a[i]:=z[i];
end;
(* q gets p with one bit changed *)
q:=p;
j:=rand(128); (* Select a random bit *)
q[j]:=q[j] XOR 1; (* Change it *)
z[0]=q;
(* encrypt q *)
for i:=1 to 16 do
begin
        b[i]:=round(i, z[i-1]);
        b[i]:=z[i];
end;
(* Compute the Hamming distance after each round *)
for i:=1 to 16 do
begin
        x[i]:=a[i] XOR b[i];
        HammingDistance[i]:=0;
        for j:=1 to 128 do
        begin
          if x[i,j]=1 then
            HammingDistance[i]:=HammingDistance[i]+1;
        end;
end;
```

Algorithm 3: A single iteration of the Avalanche security experiment

1,000,000,000 iterations		
round	mean no. of changed bits	std. dev.
1	4.968691	4.716022
2	25.012033	21.593347
3	51.343544	18.757178
4	62.762050	7.992395
5	63.961569	5.772046
6	63.999039	5.660274
7	63.999970	5.656852
8	63.999882	5.656703
9	64.000334	5.656869
10	64.000131	5.656611
11	64.000128	5.656791
12	63.999911	5.656750
13	64.000166	5.656684
14	63.999978	5.656894
15	63.999925	5.656738
16	63.999935	5.656885

Table 3: Avalanche experiment results

```
for i=1 to 128 do
        indata[i]:=random(2);
out1:=encrypt(in, key);
indata[bit]=indata[bit] XOR 1;
out2:=encrypt(indata, key);
for i=1 to 128 do
        diffs[i]=diffs[i]+ (out1[i] XOR out2[i]);
```

Algorithm 4: Differential Analysis Iteration

200,000,000 iterations

bit changed	output bit	number of diffs	bias
27	4	99,974,841	0.000126
120	93	99,975,279	0.000124
24	49	99,975,688	0.000122
69	76	99,976,104	0.000119
107	100	99,976,126	0.000119
26	9	99,976,409	0.000118
126	92	99,976,965	0.000115
51	26	99,977,006	0.000115
51	13	100,026,422	0.000132
111	37	100,026,345	0.000132
43	6	100,025,820	0.000129
68	85	100,025,637	0.000128
23	67	100,025,514	0.000128
127	68	100,025,364	0.000127
83	109	100,024,344	0.000122
50	31	100,023,897	0.000119

Table 4: Differential analysis results for Pineapple

changed bit 1	changed bit 2	output bit	iterations	differences	bias
67	20	112	10,000,000	4,992,202	0.000780
57	30	26	10,000,000	4,992,419	0.000758
48	12	9	10,000,000	4.992,560	0.000744
126	117	97	10,000,000	4,992,620	0.000738
120	68	79	10,000,000	5,007,236	0.000724
40	23	127	10,000,000	4,992,799	0.000720
114	37	96	10,000,000	5,007,172	0.000717
72	56	99	10,000,000	4,992,850	0.000715
75	20	62	10,000,000	4,992,858	0.000714
46	18	96	10,000,000	4,992,917	0.000708
81	33	37	10,000,000	4,992,969	0.000703
92	7	24	10,000,000	4,992,993	0.000701
121	82	20	10,000,000	5,007,005	0.000700
123	121	60	10,000,000	5,007,000	0.000700
25	14	56	10,000,000	4,993,055	0.000695
121	105	1	10,000,000	4,993,080	0.000692

Table 5: Top 2-bit Differential Results

4.5 Dragonfire Cipher

The Pineapple Cipher was introduced as a precursor and primitive for the Dragonfire Cipher, which we will describe in this section. We will use the Pineapple Cipher with a key of zeros as a primitive in the initialization of Dragonfire. Any permutation can be used as long as it is complete and shows the avalanche property. The Dragonfire cipher is more secure than Pineapple because of a better key-scheduling algorithm and because it has keyed S-boxes. Where the Pineapple Cipher uses fixed S-boxes, the Dragonfire Cipher chooses S-boxes as a function of the key. In effect, the Dragonfire cipher selects among 2^{64} different possible ciphers based on the key. Dragonfire encryption speeds should be similar to Pineapple encryption speeds. A test was done on an Opteron processor in which Dragonfire encrypted 12 megabits per second for sixteen seconds. On the Athlon X2 64 4000+ processor on which Pineapple encrypted 11,750 kbits/second, Dragonfire encrypted 7,288 kbits/second. The difference between these speeds may be best explained by the operation of the memory hierarchy in storing the subkeys. While the Pineapple subkeys can be stored in registers as they are stepped through, the Dragonfire subkeys are expanded to 1024 bits. This means that the cache must be accessed an extra eight times for each Dragonfire round.

Many cryptanalytic methods use precomputations based on the S-boxes. This can be made considerably more difficult by varying the S-boxes between sessions. To vary the S-boxes, the encryption program can keep a table of generators for the selected Fermat prime and use hashes of the key as indices into this table. This technique is used in the Dragonfire cipher.

After the key is established, S-boxes can be generated from these generators. While this increases the setup time for the cipher, it makes cryptanalytic methods based on precomputed statistical tables which are dependent on the S-boxes considerably more difficult. We also do more processing on the subkeys resulting in a desirable security property. We show in Theorem 1 that the subkeys are pseudo-independent. This means that discovering bits of a subkey does not lead to other bits of the subkeys as seen in Definition 1 on page 66. We achieve this property by encrypting them using Pineapple and a known key.

The Dragonfire cipher computes a 64-bit hash of the key to generate the S-boxes. By hash, we mean a function $h : x \rightarrow y$ such that $|x|$ is variable and $|y|$ is fixed. The hash function for choosing the generators should be hard to invert.

We call the technique of choosing each S-box from a list of S-boxes with known properties *polymorphism* making Dragonfire S-boxes *polymorphic S-boxes* (see Figure 6). Polymorphic S-boxes are novel to Dragonfire. In the Dragonfire design, the preselected S-boxes are computed using exponentiation modulo 257 as in Pineapple. Each byte of the hash represents an S-box, 7 bits give the generator, and one bit rotates the table values (see Figure 7).

Selecting S-boxes requires additional initialization for the Dragonfire cipher as shown in Algorithm 5. The function $p(x)$ represents applying the Pineapple cipher to x with a key of zeros. The encryption algorithm differs slightly from Pineapple and is shown in Algorithm 6 on page 65. Where Pineapple schedules the key in its encryption algorithm, Dragonfire uses a pre-scheduled key from the initialization algorithm.

The subkeys are derived from encryptions of the key. This is key to achieving the pseudo-independence property. In fact, in order to learn any bits of the key from the subkey, two adjacent subkeys must be completely known. This is because each bit of the two adjacent subkeys depends on all 128-bits of the original key that correspond to the two subkeys and vice versa (see Figure 8 on page 63)

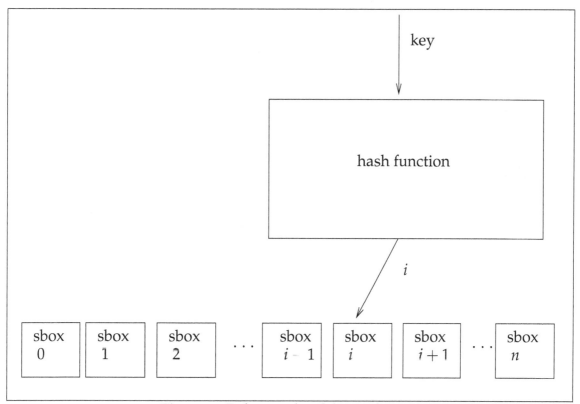

Figure 6: Polymorphic S-box selection

through the avalanche property of the Pineapple cipher. This reduces the effectiveness of cryptanalytic attacks such as differential cryptanalysis that discover bits of the subkeys. The key scheduling algorithm is illustrated in Figure 8.

Decryption is accomplished by running through the encryption steps in reverse order using inverses of the S-boxes in place of the S-boxes. Inverses of the S-boxes can be obtained by swapping the index into the S-box with its value.

If the S-boxes of a Dragonfire encryption are compromised, it is still not immediately obvious to the cryptanalyst based on this information what the key is, but the security may be reduced by 64 bits because this is the amount of information contained in the selection of the S-boxes. By XORing and truncating the results of the p-function, the security of the keys generating the S-boxes is preserved. The key, k, is broken up into 128-bit words, $k_1, k_2, \cdots$. A hash, $h(k)$, is computed as fol-

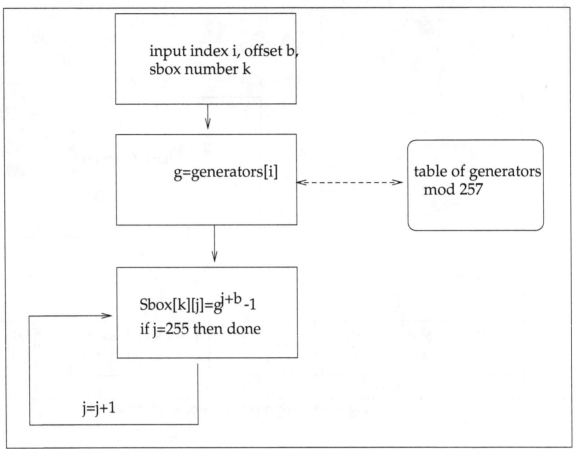

Figure 7: S-box generation for Dragonfire

lows, $h(k) = p(k_1) \oplus p(k_2) \oplus \cdots$. The first sixty-four bits of $h(k)$ are used to choose the S-boxes. This is hard to invert because the XORs lose information. Clearly, if the S-boxes are discovered, their value does not completely determine what any of the bits of the key are. Blowfish, on the other hand, requires the S-boxes to remain secret but is not known to be less secure than ciphers with open S-boxes.

The subkeys for Dragonfire are generated from the key using Pineapple so that discovery of a bit of a subkey does not result in the discovery of bits of other subkeys. We call this property *pseudo-independence* (see Definition 1) and this makes cryptanalytic techniques which yield individual bits of subkeys more difficult. More efficient cryptanalytic methods than exhaustive key search often learn the values of bits of subkeys and use those to determine bits of other subkeys and bits of the key. Pseudo-independence makes it so that it is necessary to learn two or more complete subkeys in order to learn any bits of the key or bits of other sub-keys. This allows us to be flexible in key sizes, allowing 256-bit, 384-bit, 512-bit, 768-bit, and 1024-bit keys.

There is a theoretical lower bound on a type of method known as the *black-box method* for $NP \cap coNP$ of $\Omega(2^{n/3})$ for quantum Turing machines [BBBV97]. This means that if a black-box method is used to break the cipher, the work factor may be as little as one-third of the classical work factor for that key. Thus if a 128-bit key gives a sufficient work factor to stop an ordinary adversary then a 384-bit key gives a sufficient work factor against quantum computers using black-box algorithms that are not yet known. Likewise, 768-bit keys give a post-quantum work factor equivalent to 256-bit keys.

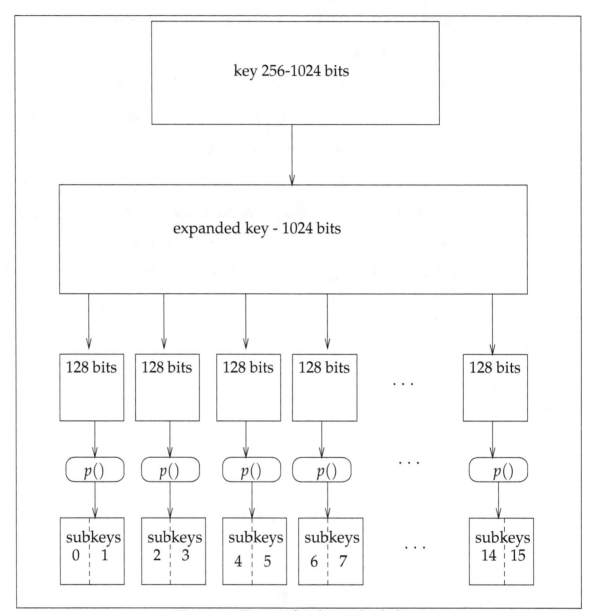

Figure 8: Dragonfire key scheduling

```
Input:   byte key[]
Output:   byte enc_S_box[8][256], byte dec_S_box[8][256]


if keylength=256    then step:=32 else
if keylength=384    then step:=48 else
if keylength=512    then step:=64 else
if keylength=768    then step:=96 else
if keylength=1024 then step:=128 else
error;
doublekey:=key concat key;
hashkey=p(key[0..128]) XOR p(key[129..255])
        [XOR p(key[256..383] [XOR p(key[384..511])
        [XOR p(key[512..767]) [XOR p(key(768..1023)]]]];
for k:=0 to 7 do
begin
        b:=hashkey[k*8];
        int c:=b shift right 7;
        b:=b AND 127;
        int g:=gens[b];
        for i:=0 to 255 do
                enc_S_box[k][i]:=expmod257(g, i+c)-1;
        for j:=0 to 255 do
                dec_S_box[k][enc_S_box[number][j]]:=j;
end;
for k:=0 to 7 do
begin
        subkeys[k*128..((k+1)*128)-1]:=
                p(doublekey[k*step..127+k*step]);
end;
```

Algorithm 5: Additional initialization for Dragonfire

```
Input:  k, p
Output: c


L := p[0]..p[63];
R := p[64]..p[128];
B := subkeys;
        for i:=1 to 16 do
        begin
                L := L  XOR (B[0]..B[63]);
                ROTATE B left 64 bits;
                for j=1 to 8 do
                begin
                 L[8j+0]..L[8j+7] := S[j][L[8j+0]..L[8j+7]];
                end;
                R := L XOR R;
                SWAP L,R;
        end;
c[0]..c[63]  := L;
c[64]..c[127] := R;
```

Algorithm 6: Dragonfire encryption algorithm

Definition 1. Suppose we are given three bit strings, k, s_1, and s_2 such that $s_1 = f(k)$ and $s_2 = g(k)$, where f and g can be computed in polynomial time by a deterministic Turing Machine and $|s_1| = |s_2|$. We denote the probability of a value v being completely determined by $\mathbf{Pr}(\det(v))$. By completely determined, we mean that the value remains constant for all possible values of unknown values. We say that s_1 and s_2 are *pseudo-independent* if both of the following statements are true:

1. The maximum probability over all i for the ith bit of k to be completely determined given less than all of the bits of s_1 or s_2 is: $\mathbf{Pr}(\det(k_i)) < \frac{1}{|k|}$.

2. The maximum probability over all i that the ith bit of s_1 can be completely determined given only s_2 is: $\mathbf{Pr}(\det(s_{1,i})) < \frac{1}{|s_1|}$.

      ∎

If a group of strings is pairwise pseudo-independent then the strings can be reversed, so the following property also holds. The maximum probability that a bit of s_2 can be determined given only s_1 is: $\mathbf{Pr}(\det(s_{2,i})) < \frac{1}{|s_2|}$.

The property in the following theorem that no invariants other than the number of bits holds for the outputs over all of the inputs follows from the fact that p and p^{-1} are permutations. What this property means is that we do not have any information such as parity or the number of zeros or other invariant properties of the output regardless of the input. Since all bit strings of length 128 are valid inputs for p and p^{-1} and these functions are permutations, all bit strings of length 128 are output for some input. This precludes any invariant other than the number of bits.

Theorem 1. *If p and p^{-1} are complete, show the avalanche effect, and do not lead to invariant properties over all the inputs for all the outputs other than the number of bits, then the subkeys of Dragonfire are pairwise pseudo-independent.*

Proof: Assume p and p^{-1} are complete and show the avalanche effect. Also, assume that the bits which are assumed to be known in this proof are the only information known about the values of variables—i.e., that an analyst does not have information such as parity or number of zeros. This is true because the hash function does not have invariant properties on the output. This allows an information-theoretic proof. In order to show that the subkeys of Dragonfire are pair-wise independent, we must show that for any pair of subkeys of Dragonfire, properties (1) and (2) of Definition 1 hold. In understanding the proof, it may help to refer to Figure 8 on page 63. Bear in mind that $y = p(x)$ is complete and shows the avalanche effect, so changing a single bit of x changes each bit of y with probability $\frac{1}{2}$. The same is true for p^{-1}.

(1) Since $y = p^{-1}(x)$ is complete and shows the avalanche effect, consider the probability that a bit of y remains unchanged for all possible values of one undetermined input bit. This is $1/2$ by the avalanche effect. For two possible input bits, it is $(1/2)(1/2) = 1/4$. In general, if j bits of x are not determined, there are 2^j possible values of y, because these j bits are variables that each may take on a value of 0 or 1. Since the avalanche effect states that the probability of either value for a bit for each of these values is equal, this means that the probability that a bit of y remains constant under all combinations of j bits is $1/2^j$. Since h^{-1} has the avalanche and completeness properties, the probability of determining a bit of the key even if s_1 and s_2 are completely known is at most 2^{-64} as there are 64 unknown bits for each block. This satisfies the first condition as $2^{-64} < \frac{1}{1024}$ and $|k| = 1024$.

(2) Suppose that all the bits of the subkey s_2 are known. Then there are two possibilities: either s_1 and s_2 are generated by the same bits of k or they are not. First, let us consider the case where they do not. (See Figure 9 on the next page).

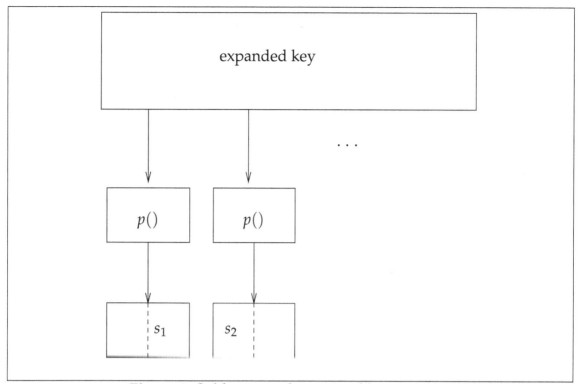

Figure 9: Subkeys not determined by same bits

Suppose that the bits of k which determine s_2 are known. The maximum number of bits of k which s_1 and s_2 share is then 32. That means that there are $2^{64-32} = 2^{32}$ possible values of s_1 for this value of s_2. The probability of any given bit of s_1 being fixed by this value of s_2 is then $1/2^{32}$. $|s_1| = 64$ and $2^{-32} < \frac{1}{64}$. This satisfies the second condition of the definition.

Now let us consider the case where s_1 and s_2 are determined by the same bits of k (see Figure 10 on the following page). Suppose, further, that we know all the bits of s_2. Then there are 2^{64} possible values of the bits of k which determine s_1 and s_2. That means that each bit of s_1 has a probability of remaining constant under all these combinations with probability $2^{-64} < \frac{1}{64}$. This satisfies the second condition of the definition.

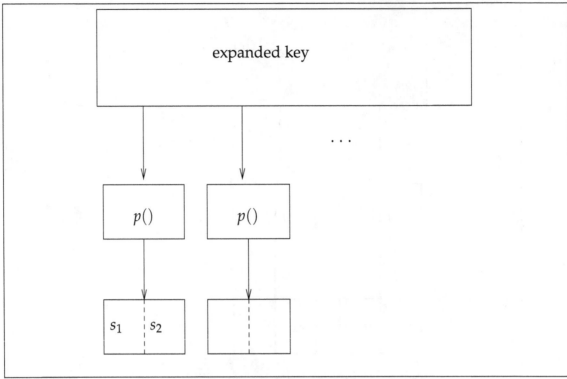

Figure 10: Subkeys determined by same bits

4.6 Pseudorandom Number Generator

We need a pseudorandom number generator in Chapter 5. In this section, we define the Dragonfire PRNG. The Dragonfire PRNG has the advantage that it can be configured to have cryptovariables whose total number of bits is sufficient for post-quantum security. The pseudorandom number generator is built from the Dragonfire cipher. The cryptovariables for the PRNG are the key, the mask, and the initialization vector (IV). The key may optionally be used to generate subkeys which are required for post-quantum security. Subkeys are derived from the encryption key and XORed with the half-blocks in the same manner as Dragonfire. The mask and the IV form the seed and are the inputs to the algorithms for generating random bits. The key is used at initialization time to generate the S-boxes using the Dragonfire initialization routine in Algorithm 5 on page 64.

There are two algorithms for pseudorandom number generation corresponding to two modes: fast and secure. The secure method is given in Algorithm 7 on page 71. The fast algorithm is given in Algorithm 8 on page 72. If a mask is not specified the default mask is: F1 54 03 92 E4 C2 BD 32 D1 23 63 F1 29 25 5E AA. The reason for specifying the mask is to prevent the unlikely situation where the high bits of the key bytes are zero and the IV is zero. Without a mask, this would lead to the generator always producing zero if the subkeys are not used. If the mask is secret it provides additional security against learning the IV from the bits that are output.

For post-quantum security, the key may be used to generate subkeys using the Dragonfire initialization scheme. If this is done, the subkeys are XORed in the algorithm in the same manner as Dragonfire.

Randomness tests were conducted on both random number generation modes. The secure mode and fast mode p-values are in the same range. This suggests that either mode gives good statistical randomness based on these measures. The advantage of using secure mode over fast mode is that it is much harder for an analyst to determine the cryptovariables such as the initialization vector. This is because much less information is revealed in each application. The NIST battery of tests [RSN+01] was run on the secure mode, the fast mode and 3DES. It should be noted that the source code for the tests was old and we were not able to compile and run many of the tests. All the tests that we were able to run were successful except for the Fast Fourier Transform test. 3DES also failed that test, suggesting a problem with the Fast Fourier Transform test. In Table 6 on the next page we show the tests that ran without a fatal program error on our installation.

```
Input:  byte iv[16], mask[16];
Output: bit

p:=iv XOR mask;
for l:=1 to 16 do
begin
  L := p[0]..p[63];
  R := p[64]..p[128];
  B := k;
  for i:=1 to 16 do
  begin
    L := L XOR (B[0]..B[63]);
    ROTATE B left 16 bits;
    for j=1 to 8 do
       L[8j+0]..L[8j+7] := S[j][L[8j+0]..L[8j+7]];
    R := L XOR R;
    SWAP L,R;
  end;
  c[0]..c[63] := L;
  c[64]..c[127] := R;
end;
iv=c;
bit:=c[0] XOR c[64];
```

Algorithm 7: DragonFire PRNG secure

test	secure p-value	fast p-value	3DES
block-frequency	0.990675	0.758270	0.757018
cumulative sums (1)	0.612388	0.626252	0.073236
cumulative sums (2)	0.733891	0.502622	0.329148
fft	0.002777	0.006648	0.008033
frequency	0.596805	0.381574	0.170843
stats (1)	0.581102	0.710089	0.516578
stats (2)	0.268324	0.192640	0.939444

Table 6: Results from NIST tests on Dragonfire PRNG

```
Input:   byte iv[16], mask[16];
Output:  bits[64]

p:=iv XOR mask;
for l:=1 to 16 do
begin
  L := p[0]..p[63];
  R := p[64]..p[128];
  B := k;
  for i:=1 to 16 do
  begin
    ROTATE B left 16 bits;
    L := L  XOR (B[0]..B[63]);
    for j=1 to 8 do
       L[8j+0]..L[8j+7] := S[j][L[8j+0]..L[8j+7]];
    R := L XOR R;
    SWAP L,R;
  end;
  c[0]..c[63]  :- L;
  c[64]..c[127] := R;
end;
iv=c;
bits[0..63]:=c[0] XOR c[64]..c[63] XOR c[127]
```

Algorithm 8: DragonFire PRNG fast

4.7 Discussion

Methods of building S-boxes should be hard to embed trapdoors in. The specific method used for Pineapple and Dragonfire has properties desirable in a cipher and does not immediately yield to differential cryptanalysis. There are other forms of cryptanalysis which may be tried including linear [OA94, HKM95, BCQ04], bilinear [Cou04], and algebraic attacks [MR02].

The Pineapple cipher follows the design patterns and values of other successful ciphers. It follows the design values of diffusion and confusion with the proven Feistel architecture. The S-boxes are based on group exponentiation so equations to model the cipher are highly non-linear. The cipher most similar to Pineapple is

SAFER.

Using Pineapple's method of obtaining S-boxes and its general design, 2^{56} different ciphers may be built. If we also add the option of rotating each S-box by one, this brings the number to 2^{64} S-boxes. This means that if we select the S-boxes based on a key, then this has the effect of having this many different ciphers depending on the key. Using this insight, we have constructed a cipher with polymorphic S-boxes, which we call the Dragonfire Cipher.

The Dragonfire cipher has the advantages of Pineapple and keyed S-boxes. Keyed S-boxes also gives it the advantages of Blowfish. Most cryptanalysis methods require the precomputation of tables that depend on the S-boxes. By changing the S-boxes with each session, the precomputation of these tables becomes impractical. A cryptanalyst would have to precompute 2^{64} tables to account for the different possibilities. Dragonfire also has pseudo-independent subkeys which further increase the difficulty of cryptanalysis. The cipher most similar to Dragonfire is Twofish which also has both keyed S-boxes and subkeys which are hashed from the key using a function that prevents one from learning bits of key from only a few bits of subkey. Unlike Twofish, the S-boxes in Dragonfire are balanced and have predictable security properties.

Chapter 5

Secure Set Membership Using 3SAT

The most popular computational foundation for cryptographic security is hardness assumptions based on number-theoretic problems such as factoring, discrete logarithm, and elliptic logarithm [DH76, RSA78, BF03]. These problems are all related, so if one is broken it is likely that they all will be broken. (See [dM04] for further discussion of this.) Their security is not proven and is likely to either remain unproven or be broken. They are also vulnerable to quantum attacks, such as those pioneered by Shor [Sho94]. It is desirable to have many kinds of cryptographic primitives whose security is based on a wide array of unrelated assumptions, so that if one system is compromised, they are not necessarily all compromised. In this chapter, we present a system based on an alternative logic-based assumption that does not appear to be closely related to these other assumptions.

Specifically, we consider the use of the well known Boolean satisfiability problem to provide a very general cryptographic primitive, *secure set membership*. Secure set membership can be used to provide digital credentials, with or without identification, as well as for some signature problems such as timestamping. For example, consider a system for maintaining encrypted PINs for credit cards. Each credit card may have multiple PINs (for multiple users); any solution should hide the PINs in such a way that the system accepts valid PINs, but nobody can determine any valid PIN that he does not already know. If the system is used in a setting in which it is reasonable for the system to be able to determine which user it is talking to, then it is possible for the system to simply store hashes of all the valid PINs and compare a received hashed PIN with this list to determine if it is valid. This is an example of *credentials with identification*. However, if the users of the credit card do not want to identify themselves, or if the credit card issuer prefers to have users not identify themselves, except as a valid user of the credit card in question, when they make a purchase, then this results in the goal of *anonymous credentials*. For anonymous credentials, the user wants to prove that he has valid credentials without giving the credentials away.

In this chapter, we provide a means for constructing a secure set membership system that can be used both for credentials with identification and for anonymous credentials. Secure set membership can be used as an alternative to digital signatures for some applications including timestamping [BdM94]. We note that our system has the desirable property that each participant can choose her own set elements. In the setting of digital credentials, this allows participants to choose their credential values (rather than having them determined by a third party or as an output of a distributed credential generation algorithm), thus making the system suitable for use with credentials that are determined by user-chosen passwords or biometrics.

Our proposed solution is based on the Boolean satisfiability problem (SAT), which has not previously been used for digital credentials. We are aware that the use of the problem of finding witnesses for 3SAT instances as a security assumption is unusual and the practice of basing cryptographic hardness on *NP-*

completeness is shaky in general, because the worst case hardness required for *NP*-completeness does not say anything about most cases or the expected case. However, we think it is of interest nonetheless. First, algorithmic advances and new computing models threaten many of the commonly used cryptographic assumptions, such as the hardness of factoring. Secondly, SAT is perhaps one of the most studied *NP*-complete problems, and a fair bit is known about how to choose instances that appear to be hard. We discuss this further in Section 5.3.4 and Section 5.5 in the context of our proposed solution.

Our contribution includes three protocols with applications to anonymous credentials, credentials with identification, accounts with multiple users, and digital timestamping. Specifically, we provide a method for generating representations of sets of provided elements. We also provide a method of using a resulting representation to prove a particular element was in the set at the time the representation was generated and a method of using the representation to show a party holds a valid set element without revealing the element itself. Our representations are random 3SAT instances of a particular form that accept the chosen witnesses. We show (Theorem 2) that among 3SAT instances that accept the selected witnesses and have the selected number of clauses, the algorithm chooses one uniformly at random. The security of the scheme relies on the computational difficulty of finding satisfying assignments to such 3SAT instances. Our system has the following properties:

- It generates instances of 3SAT that are satisfied by a given set of strings.

- It generates any suitable instance of 3SAT with equal probability. This is shown in Theorem 2.

- In combination with zero knowledge proofs for 3SAT, it provides interactive proofs that can be used for anonymous credentials.

- Assuming the 3SAT instances generated are appropriately hard, it provides security against an attacker either finding a participant's element from the information needed to verify set membership or finding other bit strings that satisfy the set membership problem.

We discuss some related work in Section 5.1. We define the set membership problem in Section 5.2. We present our system in Section 5.3. In Section 5.4, we discuss applications, including anonymous credentials and digital timestamping. We conclude with further discussion in Section 5.5.

A preliminary version of this work appeared in the Proceedings of the Eighth International Conference on Information and Communications Security (ICICS 2006) [dMW06].

5.1 Related Work

The set membership problem was first addressed by Benaloh and de Mare with one-way accumulators in 1993 [BdM94]. A number of schemes based on one-way accumulators were developed including schemes for digital credentials [CL02, BP97]. The schemes for credentials typically differ from the other schemes, which tend to concentrate on the idea of a distributed signature, in several ways. These include central authorities in the credential scheme, as well as support of additional properties such as revocation. All these schemes depend on the difficulty of the RSA problem for their security.

Another approach to set membership is to use Merkle trees or similar tree-based methods to store the elements of the set [Mer82, Mer88, BdM91]. In these methods, each participant retains a certificate and her own set element. In effect, each element of the set is signed by a central authority. However, these methods are either not storage-efficient or require more than a constant amount of time to check relative to the number of entries [Szy04].

In a credential system, members of the credentialed group have, or are given, credentials that they can use to prove their membership in the set of authorized persons, without revealing which of the members they are. Biometric data may be used to prevent transferability of credentials, together with zero knowledge proofs of knowledge, for a group member to prove to a verifier that she holds a valid credential without revealing it. Anonymous credentials have been widely studied and solutions based on various cryptographic assumptions have been given (e.g. [CL01, CL02, Acq03, IM03]).

Several approaches have been taken to digital credentials. Most of these approaches require a central authority (such as [BdM94, CL02]), though some approaches based on one-way accumulators do not require a central authority. Our approach can work with or without a central authority. The combination of one-way accumulators and zero-knowledge proofs was introduced by Camenisch and Lysyanskaya [CL02]. Other credential systems allow revocation of anonymity (e.g. Camenisch and Lysyanskaya [CL01]).

Our work makes use of the assumed computational difficulty of finding satisfying assignments to certain kinds of satisfiable 3SAT instances. A related use of the hardness of SAT for achieving security has been recently proposed for hiding information in anomaly detection applications [EAFH04, EFH04a, EFH04b, Esp05]. Their work is concerned with maintaining lists of information that, if compromised, will not compromise the larger system for applications such as intrusion detection. The central idea of our system is to represent an element of a set by an assignment to a set of variables, and the set of elements by a 3SAT instance that is satisfied by the corresponding assignments. In comparison, the work of Esponda et al. uses a SAT instance to represent a database; in their case, they represent the values *not* in the database by satisfying assignments.

We note that both our use of 3SAT and Esponda et al.'s use of SAT do not have the same difficulties as with earlier use of *NP*-complete problems for cryptography, such as the knapsack problem (see [Odl90] for a nice survey of this history), because it is not necessary to embed a trapdoor to be used for operations such as decryption.

The idea of developing post-quantum cryptosystems and cryptographic tools has received some attention recently [OTU00, KLC$^+$00, LLK$^+$06, HPS98, Cou01, FJ03]. Most of these results deal with public-key cryptography and key-exchange. One method that has received much attention, a system based on braid groups, may be weak [MSU06]. There is more discussion of related post-quantum systems in Section 2.3 on page 13.

5.2 Preliminaries

In this section, we define the secure set membership problem. A *secure set membership system* consists of two parts. First, the set must be established. Later, holders of set elements can prove their elements' set membership to others. Depending on the application, it may be desirable for the proof to reveal the set element or to keep it secret. Specifically, we have the following definitions.

Definition 2. A *set establishment protocol* is a protocol carried out by some number m of *participants* $P_1, \ldots, P_m$. Each P_i holds as input *set element* w_i. The output of the protocol is a *set representation* $T = T(w_1, \ldots, w_m)$. ∎

In our system, the set establishment protocol also takes a string of random bits which guide its nondeterministic choices. Thus the function looks like: $T = T(r, w_1, \ldots, w_m)$ where r is a string of random bits.

Definition 3. A *set membership protocol* is a protocol carried out by a participant P holding a set element w and a *verifier* V holding a set representation T. An honest verifier accepts if and only if the representation T was generated from a set of elements including w, even if P is cheating. The verifier learns w. ∎

Obviously, the set membership protocol is unsuitable for credential systems in which the set elements are reusable credentials, because it allows both V (and possibly eavesdroppers) to learn w and thereby to masquerade as P in the future to others. The protocol is also unsuitable for anonymous credential systems unless further measures are taken, because it allows V to distinguish between different provers because they have differing credentials. Fortunately, both of these difficulties can be eliminated by using a proof of possession protocol, defined below, instead of a set membership protocol.

Definition 4. A *proof of possession protocol* is a protocol carried out by a participant P holding a set element w and a verifier V holding a set representation T. An honest verifier accepts if and only if the representation T was generated from a set of elements including w, even if P is cheating. The verifier V does not learn w, even if V is cheating. The verifier, with no information other than the set representation and the knowledge that the prover has a valid element of the set, can simulate the prover, generating the same transcript as would be generated by the valid interaction between the prover and verifier. We call this property *zero knowledge* (see Section 3.5). ∎

In Definition 4, we assume all participants are computationally bounded. The elements of the set are interpreted as assignments to a set of variables. We call these assignments *witnesses*, because they will become witnesses to the satisfiability of 3SAT expressions. Our solutions depend on the computational infeasibility of finding witnesses for certain 3SAT expressions (also called *instances*). We discuss the validity of this assumption further in Section 5.3.4.

When we discuss a 3SAT instance, we pay attention to two parameters. These are the number, ℓ, of variables, and the number, n, of clauses, which is also called the *size* of the instance. We also consider the *clause density* $\alpha = \frac{n}{\ell}$, which is an important parameter for determining the difficulty of a 3SAT instance [ABS03]. We refer to a 3SAT instance that represents the set of elements as a *set representation* or, when clear from context, simply as a *set*.

5.3 Secure Set Membership

In this section, we describe our secure set membership protocols. We first describe in Section 5.3.1 a centralized process for a trusted party to establish a set representation for a set of given elements. In Section 5.3.2, we describe a distributed version of the set establishment protocol, which can be carried out by the participants holding set elements and does not require a centralized trusted party. In Section 5.3.3, we describe how to show set membership for elements of the established set. We discuss the security of our solutions in Section 5.3.4.

5.3.1 Centralized Set Establishment Protocol

Let $W = \{w_1, w_2, \cdots, w_m\}$ be a set of assignments to ℓ variables, $\{v_1, \ldots, v_\ell\}$. Each w_i represents an individual element. The trusted party, say $\mathcal{T}$, generates a set representation for W—that is, a 3SAT instance satisfied by each $w_i \in W$. To do this, $\mathcal{T}$ repeatedly generates random clauses that are the conjunction of 3 literals over variables in V. $\mathcal{T}$ checks each clause generated to determine whether it is satisfied by every $w_i \in W$. If there is some $w_i \in W$ that does not satisfy the clause, then $\mathcal{T}$ discards the clause and randomly selects a replacement clause which goes through the same test. Once n satisfied clauses are found, where n is a security parameter representing the desired size of the expression, their conjunction forms the desired set representation T, which is output by $\mathcal{T}$. The complete algorithm is given in Algorithm 9.

Note that the output T is an instance of the 3SAT problem satisfied by the assignments that the participants have specified as elements. It may also be satisfied by some other unknown assignments. However, even if there are such spurious witnesses, that does not mean they are easy for an attacker to find. Nonetheless, it seems desirable to avoid having many such spurious witnesses. One can reduce the number of spurious witnesses by choosing a large n, because the probability of a given assignment satisfying a 3SAT instance decreases exponentially with the size of the instance. Specifically, n should be chosen to be large enough to satisfy three security criteria:

- The conjunction of the clauses should be satisfied by very few assignments that are not valid elements.

- The size of the conjunctive normal form (CNF) expression that is made by the clauses should be large enough that there is high probability that it is not an instance of SAT for which an efficient solution is known.

- The size of the CNF expression should be large enough that it can potentially be computationally infeasible to find satisfying assignments.

In general, this can be accomplished by choosing a suitably large number of variables and setting the clause density to a suitable value. The value for m is a parameter for the system. The value ℓ is fixed based on security requirements and the clause density is chosen to be something believed to be hard. The security of the scheme is discussed further in Section 5.3.4.

Input: A set of variable assignments $W = \{w_1, w_2, \cdots, w_m\}$ to ℓ variables and the target number n of clauses.

Output: A 3SAT instance satisfied by all $w \in W$.

While there are fewer than n clauses do:

1. Select three different random numbers $\{i_1, i_2, i_3\} \in \{1, \ldots, \ell\}$. For a pseudo-random number generator see Chapter 4.

2. Select three random bits n_1, n_2, n_3. For each bit n_j, if $n_j = 0$, the literal v_{i_j} is added to the clause; if $n_j = 1$, the literal $\neg v_{i_j}$ is added to the clause instead.

3. If another clause has the same three variables and corresponding negations and return to Step 1.

4. For each w_j do

    If, for all $i \in \{i_1, i_2, i_3\}$ $((n_i = 1$ and v_i is set in $w_j)$ or $(n_i = 0$ and v_i is not set in $w_j))$ then goto Step 1.

5. Add the clause represented by $\{(n_1, v_{i_1}), (n_2, v_{i_2}), (n_3, v_{i_3})\}$ to the instance.

Algorithm 10: A centralized protocol for establishing a set

We now turn our attention to the computational complexity of this algorithm. We note that there is some chance that the algorithm might not even terminate, if there are not a sufficient number of available clauses that satisfy the given witnesses. However, if ℓ is chosen relatively large in comparison to m, and ℓ is sufficiently large compared to m and n, there should be a sufficient number of clauses that satisfy the witnesses. In order to make sure that the algorithm will terminate we need the following condition to hold:

$$n \leq \left\lfloor 8\frac{\ell!}{(\ell - 3)!}((7/8)^m) \right\rfloor$$

The right hand side of the equation is the total number of possible clauses multiplied by the fraction of the clauses that will be accepted. This gives the number of clauses that may be included in the final instance. It is desirable to choose ℓ based on security requirements. Finding witnesses is conjectured to be exponential in ℓ. A discussion of how to choose n follows in Section 5.5.

Assuming a large number of clauses satisfy the given witnesses, consider a particular witness representing one set element and consider a single randomly chosen 3SAT clause. There are three variables in a clause, all of which are given some assignment in the witness. Each variable in the clause can appear as a literal in either positive or negative form, so there are eight possible cases. Of these, seven are satisfied by the witness; it is only not satisfied (and therefore not accepted) in the case where none of the three literals is satisfied. Thus, the probability of a clause satisfying one witness is $\frac{7}{8}$. If there are m witnesses, then the probability of a clause satisfying all of them is $(\frac{7}{8})^m$. It follows that the expected number of tries required to generate a clause in the set representation is $(\frac{8}{7})^m$. It takes $O(\log \ell)$ bits to represent a clause and the clause must be checked against m witnesses, each of which can be done in constant time. Therefore, it takes $O(m \log \ell)$ time to test a clause to determine whether it is satisfied by all the witnesses.

In order to generate n clauses, it is necessary to find n distinct clauses that are satisfied by W. As each clause is found, it becomes slightly harder to find the next clause, as duplicates will sometimes be chosen. However, as long as n is very small relative to the total number of clauses that satisfy W, this has a negligible effect. If the probability that a random chosen clause passes both tests (satisfies W and is not a duplicate) were fixed at $(\frac{7}{8})^m$, then the expected running time to generate a set representation would be $O(n((\frac{8}{7})^m)m \log \ell)$. We note that in cases where n is a significant fraction of the total number of clauses that satisfy W, then this would not be the case.

In practice, this means that it is only computationally efficient to generate an instance for at most up to around a hundred witnesses. A hundred witnesses leads to an expectation of 629,788 rejected clauses per accepted clause, easily doable with current computers. When the number of witnesses reaches a hundred and fifty, there is an expectation of about five hundred million rejected clauses for each accepted clause, probably infeasible for a typical modern computer for even a small number of clauses.

5.3.2 Distributed Set Establishment Protocol

We now discuss the distributed protocol for establishing T, which is given in Algorithm 11. This algorithm works for *honest-but-curious* participants, who are assumed to follow their specified protocols but who may pool their information to try to learn more than they are supposed to. It also has some resilience against cheating participants who do not follow the protocol; for example, cheating parties can cause an easy instance of 3SAT to be chosen, but in some cases the other participants can detect that this may be happening. At a high level, the protocol executes as follows: the participants locally generate local copies of the same random clause. Each determines if the clause is satisfied by her own witness and communicates this information to the others. If the clause is satisfied by all the witnesses, it is kept. Otherwise, it is discarded.

In order to protect the participants' witnesses from being disclosed, we use a verifiable secret-ballot election scheme by Benaloh [Ben87]. The scheme is based on *homomorphic encryption* and *secret sharing*. It operates by designating some participants as *tellers*. Participants give secret shares of their votes to the tellers. The tellers then use the homomorphic properties of the secret-sharing scheme to compute shares of the tally. They then collaborate to compute the actual tally and provide a proof to the participants that the tally was computed correctly.

In order to detect cheating of individual participants in our scheme, the tellers count the number of times that any participant votes "no" for any given clause. This can be accomplished without revealing the votes to the tellers by using the homomorphic property of the election scheme. The tellers maintain a running sum of each participant's votes and collaborate to determine that sum after a clause is chosen. If this sum exceeds a threshold value *maxreject*, then the instance is discarded and the protocol restarted from the beginning. Depending on the application setting for the protocol, it may be desirable to exclude participants who have exceeded the *maxreject* threshold some number of times from further participation. We note that even if a cheating participant succeeds in influencing the outcome of the protocol, she can neither learn another participant's witness nor cause another participant's witness to not satisfy the resulting 3SAT instance.

The goal is to choose *maxreject* high enough so that it detects cheating at levels that could lead to malicious participants being able to break the security of the result, but low enough so that it does not unnecessarily restart the protocol when no participants are cheating.

In order to heuristically determine a good value for *maxreject* for a given round, we need to know what the total number of possible clauses are. This is:

$$clauses = \left\lfloor \frac{\ell!/(\ell-3)!}{(8/7)^m} \right\rfloor$$

Define i as the current round and S as a security parameter. As a somewhat arbitrary threshold, we suggest:

$$maxreject = \left(\frac{\left(\frac{8}{7}\right)^m}{8} \cdot \frac{(S+\log n)}{8\log\frac{8}{7}} \right) \frac{clauses}{(clauses - i)}$$

which is derived as follows. As mentioned previously, the probability of a random clause satisfying a given witness is $\frac{7}{8}$. The first term of the formula for $maxreject$ is the inverse of the probability of all the witnesses being satisfied for a single clause divided by the number of them that a single witness rejects. This is not sufficient to give a useful probability of an honest run not being rejected because there are n clauses yielding a probability that all n is satisfied of 2^{-n}. We multiply by the logarithm of the number of witnesses converted to logarithm base $\frac{8}{7}$ and divide by 8 (to convert from elections to rejections) in order to bring the probability up to one half that all the clauses will be accepted. A security parameter is added in this process to bring the probability to the desired level. It is necessary to use a higher security parameter with fewer witnesses. Multiplying by the ratio between the total possible clauses and the remaining possible clauses scales the total number of clauses that may be considered to account for clauses that have already been chosen. If $i = clauses$ then there are no more clauses to add and the ratio cannot be computed.

This choice of $maxreject$ experimentally seems to be a good choice. See Figures 11 and 12. We recommend a value of S between 2 and 32. The larger values should be used with a smaller number of witnesses.

To ensure termination and also to provide some protection against multiple cheating participants colluding and "spreading out" their "no" votes in order not to individually exceed the *maxreject* threshold, it would also be a good idea to have a check in each iteration of the while loop that the loop has not been executed too many times, and to abort the protocol if this occurs.

In our set establishment protocol, the participants have a public shared source R of random or pseudorandom numbers. A theoretical model of algorithms executing with shared random information can be obtained with our notion of random clones in Section 3.2, or with the concept of random beacons [Rab83, Ben87]. Using R, each participant generates a clause as the disjunction of three elements. Since the same random source is used, all the participants generate the same clause. The participants hold a verifiable secret-ballot election. If the tally is unanimously "yes", the clause is kept; otherwise, it is rejected. If any participant votes "no", then the clause is discarded. This process is repeated until the target number n of clauses has been generated.

It is easy to verify that the output T is satisfied by all the inputs $w_1, \ldots, w_m$, so Algorithm 11 meets the definition of a set establishment protocol. Assuming that parties behave honestly, the expected number of tries to find a clause is $\left(\frac{8}{7}\right)^m$ as in the centralized protocol of Section 5.3.1.

Input: A set of variable assignments $W = \{w_1, w_2, \cdots, w_m\}$. Each w_i is known to participant P_i. All participants also know the number ℓ of variables to be used and the target number n of clauses, as well as a sufficiently long random string R. For a method of generating a pseudorandom string see Chapter 4.

Output: An instance of 3SAT that is satisfied by all participants' witnesses.

- set $i := 0$,

$$maxrejectbase := \frac{\left(\frac{8}{7}\right)^m}{8} \cdot \frac{S + \log n}{8 \log \frac{8}{7}}$$

$$clauses := \left\lfloor \frac{8\ell(\ell-1)(\ell-2)}{\left(\frac{8}{7}\right)^m} \right\rfloor$$

- While there are fewer than n clauses do:

  1. $maxreject := maxrejectbase \frac{clauses}{(clauses - i)}$, $i := i + 1$

  2. Using R, select three different variables i_1, i_2, i_3 and three flags n_1, n_2, n_3.

  3. Construct the clause where the flags denote the negation of variables.

  4. If the clause is equivalent to a clause already generated, discard it and return to Step 2.

  5. Hold a verifiable secret-ballot election (see [Ben87]) using "yes" if the clause is satisfied by the witness and "no" otherwise. If the tally is unanimously "yes", then add the clause to the instance. Otherwise, delete it. Each teller should maintain a running sum of each participant's shares of votes.

  6. return to Step 2.

- Use the homomorphic property to compute the number of "no" votes for each participant. If one or more exceeds $maxreject$, discard all the clauses.

Algorithm 11: A distributed algorithm

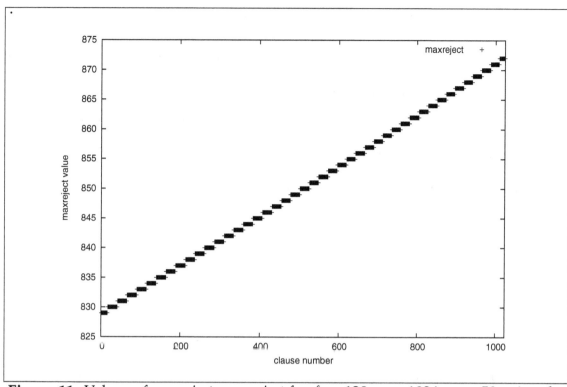

Figure 11: Values of *maxreject*: *maxreject* for $\ell = 128, n = 1024, m = 50$ using the formula in Algorithm 11

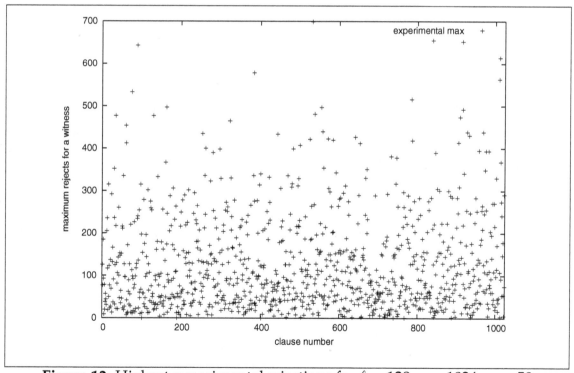

Figure 12: Highest experimental rejections for $\ell = 128, n = 1024, m = 50$

5.3.3 Set Membership

Our set representations lend themselves easily to both set membership and proof of possession protocols.

Set membership involves a participant P, who knows his element w, and a verifier V, who knows T. P wants to convince V that T was generated as a set representation that included the element w. In our case, then, P wants to convince V that w satisfies T.

A straightforward set membership protocol (in which V is allowed to communicate w to P, as per the definitions in Section 5.2), is for P to communicate w to V, who can then easily check in polynomial time whether w satisfies T. If it does, V accepts; otherwise, V rejects.

For proof of possession, it is important that the verifier never learns the credentials and cannot impersonate the prover. Fortunately, in our solution, it is not necessary to present the element to show set membership, but rather it is sufficient to prove that one knows a satisfying string. This can be done without revealing the witness via a zero knowledge proof. Assuming trapdoor one-way functions exist, then such zero knowledge proofs are possible for 3SAT using a generic construction that applies to any NP-complete problem [GMW87]. Additionally, this can be made secure against quantum computers [Wat06], in keeping with our motivation to avoid reliance on number-theoretic assumptions. If one is willing to rely on assumptions believed secure against conventional but not quantum adversaries, there are also simple examples of zero knowledge proofs for 3SAT that rely on factoring [BC87, Ben87].

5.3.4 Security

The security of the set membership protocol and the proof of possession protocol depends on the difficulty of finding witnesses that satisfy a set representation T constructed by the set establishment protocol. We show below in Theorem 2 that the representation T is random among all instances of 3SAT with n clauses and ℓ variables satisfied by the specified assignments $W = \{w_1, \ldots, w_m\}$. The instance T may possibly be satisfied by some other assignments. That is, given a set of witnesses and a specified number of clauses, there is an equal probability that our algorithm produces any instance that is satisfied by the witnesses and has the proper number of variables and clauses. The probability that T is hard is the same as the probability that it is hard to find a witness for a random such instance of 3SAT. Unfortunately, it is not known what this probability is. (In fact, if $P = NP$, then the probability is zero.)

Our system rests on the assumption that a sufficiently large random instance of 3SAT satisfying a given set of witnesses and having an appropriately chosen clause density has a high probability of being hard to solve. If this assumption holds, then it is hard for anyone to find a witness that is not an element. It is also hard for a party who does not already know an element of T to find one. These two properties provide the security for both the set membership protocol and the proof of possession protocol. In particular, for the set membership protocol, the ability for an adversary to succeed in forging a witness without overhearing one is precisely the adversary's ability to determine a satisfying assignment to T, because this property can be exactly checked by the verifier. In the case of the proof of possession protocol, the security additionally relies on the soundness of the zero knowledge proof. An adversary who cannot find a valid witness has only negligible probability of convincing the verifier to accept.

Theorem 2. *Algorithms 9 and 11 generate with equal probability any* 3SAT *instance consisting of n different clauses that is satisfied by all the assignments in W.*

Proof: The same argument applies to both Algorithm 9 and Algorithm 11, because both algorithms save or reject clauses for the same reasons.

Consider the "random algorithm," which simply has a list of all the possible instances consisting of n distinct 3-literal clauses over ℓ variables that are satisfied by all $w \in W$ and selects one instance uniformly at random.

First, we show that our algorithm generates the same set of instances as the random algorithm. Suppose a possible 3SAT instance (in the random algorithm's list) cannot be generated by our algorithm. Then a clause in it must be rejected by our algorithm either because it is a duplicate or because some assignment does not satisfy the clause. It cannot be a duplicate, as this violates the requirement for the random algorithm's list that the clauses be distinct. If some assignment does not satisfy the clause, then no instance including that clause is satisfied by the assignment. Therefore, including it would violate the condition for the random algorithm's list that it must be satisfied by W. Hence, all instances in the list drawn on by the random algorithm are candidates for generation by our algorithm.

Conversely, suppose a 3SAT instance generated by our algorithm cannot be generated by the random algorithm. Then there are two possible reasons. The first is that there is a duplicate clause resulting in the number of unique clauses being less than n. This instance cannot be generated by our algorithm because the duplicate clause will be suppressed. The other possible reason is that it is not satisfied by one of the witnesses. In this case, one of the clauses is not satisfied by that witness (as the instance is a conjunction of the clauses). This clause will be rejected by our algorithm, so this instance cannot be generated. Therefore, the set of instances selected by the random algorithm is exactly the set of instances that our algorithm can generate. Call the size of this set N.

Finally, we show that our algorithm generates each instance with the same probability as the random algorithm. The random algorithm has probability $1/N$ of choosing each of the N instances that it can generate. Our algorithm also generates each of these instances with equal probability. To see this, note that in our algorithm, each clause has a constant probability depending on how many clauses have already been chosen. The product of a fixed number of constants is a constant. Therefore all of the instances have the same probability. It follows that, for our algorithm, each clause has probability $\frac{1}{N}$, as desired.   ∎

Theorem 2 states that, given ℓ and n, the system can generate any 3SAT instance of ℓ variables with n clauses that is satisfied by the specified witnesses. We make some observations and propose some heuristic recommendations for selecting the security parameters:

- Beyond a certain threshold, increasing the number of variables without increasing the number of clauses actually reduces security because there are not enough instantiations of the variables.

- Recall that the clause density of an instance is defined as $\alpha = \frac{n}{\ell}$. Alekhnovich and Ben-Sasson [ABS03] show that if $\alpha \leq 1.63$, then the instance can be solved in linear time. They also demonstrate empirically that $\alpha < 2.5$ seems to be easy to solve. We recommend taking $\alpha \geq 8$ (i.e., choosing $n \geq 8\ell$) for security. For example, $\ell = 8,192$ and $n = 65,536$. If one is concerned about quantum attacks, then we suggest $\ell = 16,384$ and $n = 131,072$ due to the quadratic advantage given by Grover's algorithm [Gro96]. The size of the problem was selected to be the typical size of SAT-Race benchmarks and to correspond with our suggested clause density [HS00, Sin06]. These values were verified experimentally for up to ten witnesses. Systems with 20 or more witnesses were found to be insecure.

- A certain number of variables are trivial in any particular instance (i.e., because they either do not appear in positive form or in negative form, and therefore it is clear how to set them in a satisfying assignment). This can reduce the security of the system, by making it easier for an adversary to find satisfying assignments. Additionally, once the trivial variables are assigned, an adversary can then remove those clauses from consideration, potentially resulting in more trivial variables.

If our instances were random among all 3SAT instances with n clauses and ℓ variables, then the expected number of trivial variables could be limited by taking the clause density sufficiently large. However, as noted before, our instances are random only among those 3SAT instances that are actually satisfied by the set W of witnesses. Experimental results suggest that these instances are difficult for a small number of witnesses but become easier at an exponential rate as the number of witnesses is increased.

The *phase boundary* of 3SAT is the clause density at which instances go abruptly from being mostly satisfiable to mostly unsatisfiable. The 3SAT decision problem—determining whether a 3SAT instance is satisfiable or not—is believed to be hardest when instances are just above the phase boundary [HS00]. However, our problem is a little different. Our set representation instances are always satisfiable (since they are specifically chosen to satisfy a particular set of witnesses). The problem at hand for an attacker is to find a satisfying assignment. We conjecture that the problem of finding satisfying assignments for instances that are known to be satisfiable gets harder as the probability of a random instance of the same parameter being satisfiable gets smaller—i.e., well above the phase boundary.

SATLIB contains resources for experimental research on SAT and 3SAT, including the results of competitions in solving random SAT instances [HS00]. In addition, there is an annual competition to create SAT solvers called SAT-Race [Sin06]. To date, not much progress has been made on high clause-density instances. We did our experiments using the MiniSat solver which won SAT-Race 2006 and has commercial backing from Cadence Design Systems which produces formal verification tools. SAT-decision algorithms have improved tremendously in recent years on problems of interest to industrial applications such as formal verification and MiniSAT has been at the forefront of the development [ES04, EB05, EMS07, Een07]. We used the recent 2.0 version for the latest algorithms. The SAT-races, like much of the SAT literature, are concerned with the decision problem rather than the problem of finding witnesses. Finding witnesses using the decision problem as an oracle requires solving many decision problems. If even one of these problems is intractable, it may not be possible to systematically find witnesses. We also note that there is an optimization variant of the SAT problem called MAXSAT [HS00, Hås01, KZ97]. Specifically, it is possible to approximate 3SAT by finding assignments that satisfy most, but not all clauses. Known algorithms (e.g. [KZ97]) are polynomial time for finding a 7/8 assignment, but become exponential in the worst case when trying to do a full assignment. [1]

For our security experiment, we generated problems with 8,192 variables and 65,536 clauses. We found that with 20 or greater witnesses, the problems could

---

[1]For both an algorithm to compute the 7/8-approximation and a proof that MAXSAT can be solved in polynomial time if and only if $P = NP$ see Lecture 18 in [Koz06].

be decided very quickly. We generated two problems with one witness and two problems with ten witnesses. None of these four problems were decided, although they ran on a high-performance cluster for more than four weeks. In fact, when the experiment was terminated, MiniSAT reported that 0.0000% progress had been made. This suggests that our system is secure using our suggested parameters and ten or fewer witnesses, but is insecure for more witnesses than ten. It also does not help to be able to put an upper bound on the number of satisfying assignments. The unique satisfiability problem (USAT) is the SAT problem if it is known that there are no more than one satisfying assignment. Finding a solution to an instance of USAT is as hard as SAT [VV85, Koz06]. Furthermore, Valiant and Vazirani show that distinguishing between instances with no solutions or one solution is as hard as SAT.

The number of witnesses that actually satisfy the instance generated by our protocols may be greater than the number of participants. We would like to be able to check if this is the case because if we could, we could rerun the protocol until only the selected witnesses satisfy the formula. Unfortunately, counting the number of satisfying instances for a SAT problem is complete for #P, the class of counting problems [CH96]. #P (see Section 3.3 on page 29) is a hard class of problems as evidenced by the fact that a Turing machine with a #P oracle can decide the polynomial hierarchy in deterministic polynomial time, $PH \subseteq P^{\#P}$ [Tod89, Koz06]. This means that a deterministic Turing machine with an oracle that can count SAT solutions can decide languages which are Σ_k^P-complete or Π_k^P-complete for any $k \in \mathbb{N}$. NP is Σ_1^P and $coNP$ is Π_1^P (see Section 3.3) [Koz06].

Multiple cheating participants might collude to try to "spread out" their cheating rejections so that they can influence the outcome without exceeding *maxreject*. This can be compensated for by decreasing *maxreject* or by limiting the total number of rejections allowed cumulatively for all participants rather than for individual participants. However, this also increases the chance of "false positives," in which the protocol is restarted even without cheating behavior, so it is only likely to work well for a small number of colluding participants. It remains open to address other types of cheating and collusions.

5.4 Applications

There are a number of applications of the set membership problem, including credentials and document timestamping.

5.4.1 Digital Credentials

Our system applies to anonymous credentials in a fairly straightforward manner. The credentials are the elements. They are generated using either the centralized protocol or the distributed protocol and they are verified using the proof of possession protocol. In this way, the credentials are all generated at once and then the instance is distributed to the verifiers. Verifiers use the instance to anonymously determine whether a member is credentialed. If credentials with identification are desired, the member can present his witness; the verifier can then check that the witness satisfies the instance.

5.4.2 Accounts with multiple users

The system is also useful in situations where there need to be multiple authentication strings for a single account. An example is accounts with multiple users. Suppose there are three debit cards issued on one bank account and they all have the same number but each has a different PIN. The PINs can then be used as witnesses in constructing an instance. When a user wants to demonstrate that she is an authorized user of the account, she runs the proof of possession protocol using her PIN. This way, joint holders of an account can access the account without giving away their PINs (which might also be used for other accounts that are not shared).

Other applications of multiple user accounts include the use of RFID tags as witnesses in an access control system based on proximity sensors and other access control situations where it is not desirable to uniquely identify the user.

5.4.3 Access Control Lists

On some multiuser servers, such as file servers, it may be desirable to have an access control list for a resource such as a file or a directory in a format that does not immediately yield the identities of the users who may access this resource. A straightforward encoding of the users identities would yield to a dictionary attack. The user could, however, keep an access token which is only known to the user. The user could then use a set membership protocol to prove that he is in the access control list. The access control list could be extended by keeping more than one 3SAT instance. The access control list instances could be generated in a variety of ways including by the authorized parties.

5.4.4 Document timestamping

Document timestamping [BdM91, BdM94] may require a little more explanation. In document timestamping applications, we think of the distributed protocol as a distributed signature. All the parties participating in the protocol are attesting that one of their number knew each witness at the time the protocol was run by accepting the set that results from the protocol. It would not be possible for the protocol participant to execute the protocol and then choose a satisfying witness at some later date.

The timestamping system proceeds in rounds. All documents submitted during the same round are considered to be simultaneous, like patent applications arriving at the patent office on the same day. Each participant's witness is a hash of the document(s) she would like to timestamp. The distributed protocol is run, and everyone remembers the round's set, which is the timestamp. The parties may jointly publish it if they wish to allow anyone to verify a timestamp.

To verify that a document was submitted during a given round, the verifier merely needs to run the set membership protocol. The security of this system does not depend on computational security, in that if a cheating prover wishes to make his specific document appear to be timestamped and it does not satisfy the 3SAT instance, there is nothing he can do to change that. (We note, though, that in most practical settings, the adversary may be able to change his document in ways that do not affect its meaning, but do affect its encoding into a bit string, so this guarantee is not absolute.)

Digital timestamping can be used for intellectual property disputes, among other applications. In the intellectual property application, a consortium generates a timestamp with each company using a hash of the hashes of all of its documents. Each company retains the daily timestamp and publishes it for other interested parties. In a patent dispute, for instance, a party can get all the other honest participants to attest to its possession of a document on or before a certain date. This could also be used to prevent backdating in stock or other business transactions.

5.5 Discussion

We have presented a general solution to the set membership problem whose security depends on the difficulty of finding witnesses to random 3SAT instances satisfying a given set of witnesses. We have also presented applications to access control, digital credentials, and timestamping. We have shown a distributed protocol for establishing a set.

A strong justification for considering security based on 3SAT is the increased worry that advances in conventional or quantum computing may one day yield efficient algorithms for problems such as factoring and discrete logarithms typically used as a source of hardness in cryptography. It is therefore important to investigate cryptographic algorithms based on alternate (plausible) hardness assumptions to provide resilience against "breaking" of any one assumption or class of assumptions.

In 1979, Brassard showed that if a one-to-one bounded input one-way function can be shown NP-hard to invert, then $NP = \mathrm{co}NP$ [Bra79]. Our system is not one-to-one and does not meet the standard definitions of one-way functions, so Brassard's proof does not apply.

Open problems include the probability distribution of the output of our set establishment protocol with respect to all 3SAT instances. In particular, it should be investigated experimentally whether a randomly generated instance of 3SAT of size n that is satisfied by the chosen witnesses falls into one of the patterns whose solution is known to be easy, as well as determining whether all such instances can be specifically avoided.

Our protocol can be used for digital credentials including anonymous credentials, timestamping, and other set membership applications. It can also be used for applications where multiple users share an account. These include some access control and financial applications. For set membership applications like timestamping, the set representation can be thought of as a distributed signature. It can be proven to any honest participant or observer using the set membership protocol that a document was used for inclusion in the set. These applications have broad applicability to problems in cryptography and security. The advantages of this method over one-way accumulators include not needing to remember a second string and not being dependent on the factoring problem [BdM94].

As previously discussed, the expected number of clauses that must be tried to generate a clause in the set representation is $(\frac{8}{7})^m$, where m is the number of witnesses to be represented. We note that this probability depends on the number of elements and is independent of n and ℓ. In contrast, the security of the system is based on the adversary's difficulty of finding an element as a function of n and ℓ, so it may be possible to limit m so as to have efficient solutions for the participants without making the adversary's task solvable. As described earlier in Section 5.3.1, we believe that one hundred witnesses can be dealt with easily, but that as the number of witnesses begins to reach one hundred fifty, it becomes infeasible to generate an instance. It is important to remember that for our recommended parameters the system is not secure with more than ten witnesses. For the distributed protocol, the limits may be slightly lower to compensate for communication overhead. This can be countered by replacing 3SAT with k-SAT where k is $\Theta(m)$. This eliminates the exponential complexity for the participants. However, in this case, it is necessary to make α significantly greater than the phase boundary for k-SAT. It is an open problem to determine the phase boundary of k-SAT for $k > 3$.

There are also combinatorial limits to consider. The number of possible clauses for a set of witnesses is given by:

$$8\ell(\ell - 1)(\ell - 2)\left(\frac{7}{8}\right)^m$$

For $\ell = 8,192$ and $n = 65,536$, the combinatorial maximum number of witnesses is 115. We suggest 50 as a practical maximum for the distributed algorithm as the number of elections greatly increases as the system approaches its combinatorial limits. When $n = 50$, the system performs nicely, as can be seen in the experimental results in Figure 12. The values for *maxreject* are also shown in Figure 11 and were computed with $S = 2$. This worked with our choice of a seed for the random number generator so that the actual number of rejections never exceeded *maxreject*. Experimental results suggest that the system is only secure for 10 or fewer witnesses. At 20 witnesses, the system with $\ell = 8,192$ can be solved in less than a second. We could not experimentally solve systems with 10 or fewer witnesses using the MiniSat solver even with weeks of computing time on a high-performance cluster when $\ell = 8129$ and $n = 65,536$.

The space complexity for a set based on 3SAT is $\Theta(\ell \log \ell)$. For instance, a system with $8,192$ variables requires $65,536$ clauses. Altogether, this requires 128 kilobytes of storage. This space complexity is independent of the number of set elements. However, if k-SAT is used instead of 3SAT, then the space complexity grows both in the number of bits required to represent a clause and in the number of clauses required to be above the phase boundary.

Chapter 6

Conclusion

The expected emergence of quantum computers requires that new, post-quantum cryptographic primitives be developed to resist them. In this thesis we discuss post-quantum cryptography and develop two new post-quantum primitives. These primitives are believed to be secure under the quantum model if they are secure under the classical model. The first new primitive is a new symmetric-key cipher using two new cipher-design methods and the second primitive is a secure set membership primitive.

The two new cipher-design techniques in the symmetric-key cipher primitive are polymorphic S-boxes and pseudo-independent subkeys. Polymorphic S-boxes increase the challenge to the cryptanalyst by preventing the precomputation of statistical tables for the cipher and by forcing the cryptanalyst to determine what the S-boxes are. Pseudo-independent subkeys challenge the cryptanalyst by limiting the knowledge he gains from partial knowledge of subkeys. Traditionally, learning a bit of one subkey leads to bits of several other subkeys and a bit of the key. Pseudo-independent subkeys require the cryptanalyst to learn multiple complete subkeys to gain this knowledge.

The secure set membership primitive solves the secure set membership problem. Secure set membership is a generalization of the problem solved by one-way accumulators [BdM94]. Our secure set membership primitive uses a computational problem based on 3SAT which is not known to be efficiently computable by either classical or quantum computers. We show how to generate this primitive using a distributed protocol and how to prove possession of a set member without revealing the string.

The purpose of developing these two protocols is to start building the theoretical foundation for cryptography after the advent of quantum computers with many qubits. Traditional cryptography based on RSA and Diffie-Hellman can be broken by quantum computers [Sho94]. Since elliptic logarithm can be computed with a discrete logarithm oracle [MOV93], quantum computers will also break cryptography based on elliptic curves.

The secure set membership primitive is weaker than one-way functions, and cannot be used to build one-way functions or more complicated primitives. Still, it is our belief that by starting with a simple, weak primitive that more useful post-quantum primitives will be developed, possibly using our complexity assumption. Doing so will require discovering a way to generate 3SAT instances deterministically without running the risk of the cryptanalyst learning the inputs from the deterministically generated instance.

Our symmetric-key cipher is an evolution of the state of the art. The pseudo-independent subkey technique can be used in existing ciphers and polymorphic S-boxes is a promising technique for use in future ciphers. Breaking symmetric-key ciphers is asymptotically easy, but the key is chosen to be large enough to make the work factor too large for an adversary. A quantum adversary has a quadratic advantage and may even have a cubic advantage over a classical adversary [Gro96,

BBBV97]. Our cipher allows key sizes large enough to negate this advantage.

Bibliography

[ABS03]   Mikhail Alekhnovich and Eli Ben-Sasson. Linear upper bounds for random walk on small density random 3-CNFs. In *Proceedings of the 44th Annual IEEE Symposium on the Foundations of Computer Science*, 2003.

[Acq03]   Alessandro Acquisiti. Anonymous credentials through acid mixing. Unpublished manuscript, 2003.

[AD97]   Miklós Ajtai and Cynthia Dwork. A public-key cryptosystem with worst-case/average-case equivalence. In *Proceedings of the Twenty-Ninth Annual ACM symposium on Theory of Computing (STOC '97)*, pages 284–293. ACM, 1997.

[Age07]   Central Intelligence Agency. *2007 CIA World Factbook.* United States Government Printing Office, 2007.

[AGGM06]   Adi Akavia, Oded Goldreich, Shafi Goldwasser, and Dana Moshkovitz. On basing one-way functions on NP-hardness. In *Proceedings of the 38th Annual ACM Symposium on Theory of Computing (STOC '06)*. ACM Press, 2006.

[Ahl06]   Dick Ahlstrom. Quantum 'weirdness' offers huge potential. *The Irish Times*, page 15, February 23, 2006.

[AHU74]   Aho, Hopcroft, and Ullman. *The Design and Analysis of Computer Algorithms*. Addison-Wesley, 1974.

[Ajt04]   Miklos Ajtai. Generating hard instances of lattice problems. *Complexity of Computations and Proofs, Quaderni di Matematica*, 13(1-32), 2004.

[BB84a]   Charles H. Bennett and Gilles Brassard. Quantum cryptography: Public-key distribution and coin tossing. In *Proceedings of the International Conference on Computers, Systems, and Signal Processing*, 1984.

[BB84b]   Charles H. Bennett and Gilles Brassard. An update on quantum cryp tography. In *Advances in Cryptology – Crypto '84*, volume 196/1985 of *Lecture Notes in Computer Science*. Springer, 1984.

[BBBV97]   Charles H. Bennett, Ethan Bernstein, Gilles Brassard, and Umesh Vazirani. Strengths and weaknesses of quantum computing. *SIAM Journal on Computing*, 26(5):1510–1523, 1997.

[BBD$^+$99]   Eli Biham, Alex Biryukov, Orr Dunkelman, Eran Richardson, and Adi Shamir. Initial observations on skipjack: Cryptanalysis of skipjack-3xor. In *Selected Areas in Cryptography - SAC98*, volume 1556/1999 of *Lecture Notes in Computer Science*, pages 630–644, 1999.

[BC87]   G. Brassard and C. Crepeau. Zero-knowledge simulation of boolean circuits. In *Advances in Cryptography – Crypto '86*, volume 263/1987 of *Lecture Notes in Computer Science*, pages 223–233. Springer, 1987.

[BCQ04]   Alex Biryukov, Cristophe De Canniere, and Michael Quisquater. On multiple linear approximations. In *Advances in Cryptology – Crypto 2004*, volume 3152/2004 of *Lecture Notes in Computer Science*, pages 1–22. Springer, 2004.

[BCS08]   Eli Biham, Yaniv Carmeli, and Adi Shamir. Bug attacks. In *Advances in Cryptology – Crypto 2008*, volume 5157/2008 of *Lecture Notes in Computer Science*, pages 221–240, 2008.

[BdM91]   Josh Benaloh and Michael de Mare. Efficient broadcast time-stamping. Technical Report TR-MCS-91-1, Clarkson University Department of Mathematics and Computer Science, 1991.

[BdM94]   Josh Benaloh and Michael de Mare. One-way accumulators: A decentralized approach to digital signatures. In *Advances In Cryptology – Eurocrypt '93*, volume 765/1994 of *Lecture Notes in Computer Science*, pages 274–285. Springer, 1994.

[Ben87]   Josh Benaloh. *Verifiable Secret-Ballot Elections*. PhD thesis, Yale University Department of Computer Science, September 1987.

[BF03]   Dan Boneh and Matthew Franklin. Identity-based encryption from the Weil pairing. *SIAM Journal of Computing*, 32(3):586–615, 2003.

[BGS75]   Theodore Baker, John Gill, and Robert Solovay. Relativizations of the $P =?NP$ question. *SIAM Journal on Computing*, 4(4):431–442, December 1975.

[BKR97]   Johan Borst, Lars Knudsen, and Vincent Rijmen. Two attacks on reduced IDEA. In *Advances in Cryptology – Eurocrypt '97*, volume

1233/1997 of *Lecture Notes in Computer Science*, pages 1–13. Springer, 1997.

[BO88]   Ernest Brickell and A.M. Odlyzko. Cryptanalysis: a survey of recent results. *Proceedings of the IEEE*, 76/1988:578–593, May 1988.

[BP97]   Niko Baric and Birgit Pfitzmann. Collision-free accumulators and fail-stop signature schemes without trees. In *Advances in Cryptology – Eurocrypt '97*, volume 1233/1997 of *Lecture Notes in Computer Science*. Springer, 1997.

[Bra79]   Gilles Brassard. A note on the complexity of cryptography. *IEEE Transactions on Information Theory*, IT-25(2):232–233, March 1979.

[Bri84]   Ernest Brickell. Breaking iterated knapsacks. In *Advances in Cryptography – Crypto '84*, volume 196/1985 of *Lecture Notes in Computer Science*, pages 342–358. Springer, 1984.

[BS91a]   Eli Biham and Adi Shamir. Differential cryptanalysis of DES-like cryptosystems. *Journal of Cryptology*, 4(1), 1991.

[BS91b]   Eli Biham and Adi Shamir. Differential cryptanalysis of Snefru, Khafre, REDOC-II, LOKI and Lucifer (extended abstract). In *Advances in Cryptography – Crypto '91*, volume 576 of *Lecture Notes in Computer Science*, pages 156–171. Springer, 1991.

[BS93]   Eli Biham and Adi Shamir. *Differential Cryptanalysis of the Data Encryption Standard*. Springer-Verlag, 1993.

[BT03]   Andrej Bogdanov and Luca Trevisan. On worst-case to average-case reductions for np problems. In *44th IEEE Conference on the Foundation of Computer Science (FOCS 2003)*, pages 308–317. IEEE, 2003.

[BW07]   Werner Backes and Susanne Wetzel. An efficient lll gram using buffered transformations. In *Proceedings of the 10th International Workshop on Computer Algebra in Scientific Computing (CASC 2007)*, volume 4770/2007 of *Lecture Notes in Computer Science*, pages 31–44. Springer, 2007.

[CH96]   Nadia Creignou and Miki Hermann. Complexity of generalized satisfiability counting problems. *Information and Computation*, 125(1):1–12, February 1996.

[CL01]   Jan Camenisch and Anna Lysyanskaya. An efficient system for non-transferable anonymous credentials with optional anonymity revocation. In *Advances in Cryptology – Eurocrypt 2001*, volume 2045/2001 of *Lecture Notes in Computer Science*. Springer, 2001.

[CL02]   Jan Camenisch and Anna Lysyanskaya. Dynamic accumulators and application to efficient revocation of anonymous credentials. In *Advances in Cryptology – Crypto 2002*, volume 2442/2002 of *Lecture Notes in Computer Science*. Springer, 2002.

[CLRS01]   T. Corman, C. Leiserson, R. Rivest, and C. Stein. *Introduction to Algorithms*. Prentice-Hall, 2nd edition, 2001.

[Coc07]   Patrick Cockburn. Whatever happened to Ahmed Chalabi? (the man whose lies about WMD took us to war). *The Independent (London)*, 2007. May 16.

[Cor98]   Cylink Corporation. SAFER+: Cylink corporation's submission for the advanced encryption standard, August 1998. `csrc.nist.gov/encryption/aes/round1/conf1/saferpls-slides.pdf`.

[Cou01]   Nicolas T. Courtois. The security of hidden field equations (HFE). In *Proceedings of Progress in Cryptology - CT-RSA 2001: The Cryptographers' Track at RSA Conference 2001*, volume 2020/2001 of *Lecture Notes in Computer Science*. Springer, 2001.

[Cou04]   Nicolas Courtois. Feistel schemes and bi-linear cryptanalysis. In *Advances in Cryptology – Crypto 2004*, volume 3152/2004 of *Lecture Notes in Computer Science*, pages 23–40. Springer, 2004.

[CR84]   Benny Chor and Ronald L. Rivest. A knapsack type public key cryptosystem based on arithmetic in finite fields. In *Advances in Cryptography – Crypto '84*, volume 196/1985 of *Lecture Notes in Computer Science*, pages 54–65. Springer, 1984.

[CS97]   Don Coppersmith and Adi Shamir. Lattice attacks on NTRU. In *Advances in Cryptology – EUROCRYPT '97*, volume 1233/1997 of *Lecture Notes in Computer Science*. Springer, 1997.

[dB88]   Bert den Boer. Cryptanalysis of F.E.A.L. In *Advances in Cryptology – Eurocrypt '88*, volume 330/1988 of *Lecture Notes in Computer Science*, pages 293–301. Springer, 1988.

[DGS07]   Jingtai Ding, Jason E. Gower, and Dieter S. Schmidt. *Multivariate Public Key Cryptosystems*, volume 25 of *Advances in Information Security*. Springer, 2007.

[DH76]   W. Diffie and M. Hellman. New directions in cryptography. *IEEE Transactions on Information Theory*, IT-22(6):644–654, Nov. 1976.

[Din04]   Jingtai Ding. A new variant of the matsumoto-imai cryptosystem through perturbation. In *Proceedings of the 7th International Conference on Theory and Practice of Public-Key Cryptography (PKC 2004)*, volume 2947 of *Lecture Notes in Computer Science*, pages 305–318. Springer, 2004.

[dM04]   Michael de Mare. An analysis of certain cryptosystems and related mathematics. Master's thesis, State University of New York Institute of Technology, Dec. 2004.

[dM08]   Michael de Mare. Iterative symmetric-key ciphers with keyed S-boxes using modular exponentiation. Patent application 12/051,626, 2008.

[dMW06]   Michael de Mare and Rebecca N. Wright. Secure set membership using 3SAT. In *Proceedings of the Eighth International Conference in Information and Communications Security (ICICS 2006)*, volume 4307/2006 of *Lecture Notes in Computer Science*, pages 452–468. Springer, 2006.

[DR99]   Joan Daemen and Vincent Rijmen. AES proposal: Rijndael, 1999. `csrc.nist.gov/CryptoToolkit/aes/rijndael/`.

[DS05]   Jintai Ding and Dieter Schmidt. Rainbow, a new multivariable polynomial signature scheme. In *Applied Cryptography and Network Security*, volume 3531/2005 of *Lecture Notes in Computer Science*, pages 164–175, 2005.

[DS08]   Itai Dinur and Adi Shamir. Cube attacks on tweakable black box polynomials. *IACR Eprint*, (2008/385), 2008.

[DSW94]   Martin D. Davis, Ron Sigal, and Elaine J. Weyuker. *Computability, Complexity, and Languages: Fundamentals of Theoretical Computer Science*. Computer Science and Scientific Computing. Morgan Kaufmann, second edition, 1994.

[E0506]   One qubit at a time; quantum computing. *The Economist*, May 6, 2006.

[EAFH04]   Fernando Esponda, Elena S. Ackley, Stephanie Forrest, and Paul Helman. On-line negative databases. In *Proceedings of the 3rd International Conference on Artificial Immune Systems (ICARIS)*, volume 3239/2004 of *Lecture Notes in Computer Science*, pages 175–188. Springer, Sep. 2004.

[EB05]   Niklas Een and Armin Biere. Effective preprocessing in SAT through variable and clause elimination. In *Theory and Applications of Satisfiability Testing 8th International Conference (SAT 2005)*, volume 3569/2005 of *Lecture Notes in Computer Science*, pages 61–75. Springer, 2005.

[Een07]   Niklas Een. Cut sweeping. Technical report, Cadence Design Systems, 2007.

[EFH04a]   Fernando Esponda, Stephanie Forrest, and Paul Helman. Enhancing privacy through negative representations of data. Technical report, University of New Mexico, 2004.

[EFH04b]   Fernando Esponda, Stephanie Forrest, and Paul Helman. Information hiding through negative representations of data. Technical report, University of New Mexico, 2004.

[EJJ00]   Éliane Jaulmes and Antoine Joux. A chosen-ciphertext attack against NTRU. In *Advances in Cryptology – Crypto 2000*, volume 1880/2000 of *Lecture Notes in Computer Science*. Springer, 2000.

[EMS07]   Niklas Een, Alan Mishchenko, and Niklas Sörensson. Applying logic synthesis for speeding up SAT. In *Theory and Applications of Satisfiability Testing – SAT 2007*, volume 4501/2007 of *Lecture Notes in Computer Science*, pages 272–286. Springer, 2007.

[ES04]   Niklas Een and Niklas Sörensson. An extensible SAT-solver. In *Sixth International Conference on Theory and Applications of Satisfiability Testing (SAT 2003)*, volume 2919/2004 of *Lecture Notes in Computer Science*, pages 502–518. Springer, 2004.

[Esp05]   F. Esponda. *Negative Representations of Information*. PhD thesis, University of New Mexico, 2005.

[FF93]   Joan Feigenbaum and Lance Fortnow. Random self-reducibility of complete sets. *Siam Journal on Computing*, 22:994–1005, 1993.

[FGS05]   Pierre-Alain Fouque, Louis Granboulan, and Jacques Stern. Differential cryptanalysis for multivariate schemes. In *Advances in Cryptology EUROCRYPT 2005*, volume 3494/2005 of *Lecture Notes in Computer Science*, 2005.

[FJ03]   Jean-Charles Faugère and Antoine Joux. Algebraic cryptanalysis of hidden field equation (HFE) cryptosystems using Gröbner bases. In *Advances in Cryptology – Crypto 2003*, volume 2729/2003 of *Lecture Notes in Computer Science*. Springer, 2003.

[FNS75]   H. Feistel, W.A. Notz, and J.L. Smith. Some cryptographic techniques for machine-to-machine data communications. *Proceedings of the IEEE*, 63(11):1545–1554, November 1975.

[FS03]   Niels Ferguson and Bruce Schneier. *Practical Cryptography*. Wiley, 2003.

[Fum88]   Walter Fumy. On the f-function of FEAL. In *Advances in Cryptology – Crypto '87*, volume 293/1988 of *Lecture Notes in Computer Science*, pages 434–438. Springer, 1988.

[Gen01]   Craig Gentry. Key recovery and message attacks on NTRU-composite. In *Advances in Cryptology – Eurocrypt 2001*, volume 2045/2001 of *Lecture Notes in Computer Science*, pages 182–194. Springer, 2001.

[GGH97]   Oded Goldreich, Shafi Goldwasser, and Shai Halevi. Public-key cryptosystems from lattice reduction problems. In *Advances in Cryptology – CRYPTO '97*, volume 1294/1997 of *Lecture Notes in Computer Science*, pages 112–131. Springer, 1997.

[Gil98]   John Gilmore. EFF builds DES cracker that proves that data encryption standard is insecure, 1998. EFF press release.

[GJ79]   Michael Garey and David Johnson. *Computers and Intractability: A Guide to the Theory of NP-Completeness*. W.H. Freeman and Company, 1979.

[GMMU07] Robert Gilman, Alexei G. Miasnikov, Alex D. Myasnikov, and Alexander Ushakov. Report on generic case complexity. Technical report, Stevens Institute of Technology, March 2007. Algebraic Cryptography Center.

[GMW87]   Oded Goldreich, Silvio Micali, and Avi Wigderson. How to prove all NP statements in zero-knowledge and a methodology of cryptographic protocol design. In *Advances in Cryptology – Crypto '86*, volume 263/1987 of *Lecture Notes in Computer Science*, pages 171–185. Springer, 1987.

[GN08]   Nicolas Gama and Phong Nguyen. Predicting lattice reduction. In *Advances in Cryptology – Eurocrypt 2008*, volume 4965/2008 of *Lecture Notes in Computer Science*, pages 31–51. Springer, 2008.

[GOS89]   Cryptographic protection for data processing systems – cryptographic transformation algorithm – GOST 28147-89, 1989. Aleksandr Malchik (translator).

[Gro96]   Lov Grover. A fast quantum mechanical algorithm for database search. In *Proceedings of the Twenty-Eighth Annual ACM Symposium on Theory of Computing*, pages 212–219. ACM Press, 1996.

[GS02]   Craig Gentry and Mike Szydlo. Cryptanalysis of the revised NTRU signature scheme. In *Advances in Cryptology – Eurocrypt 2002*, volume 2332/2002 of *Lecture Notes in Computer Science*. Springer, 2002.

[GS07]   Guillaume and Damien Stehlè. Improved analysis of kannan's short-
              est lattice vector algorithm. In *Advances in Cryptology– Crypto 2007*,
              volume 4622/2007 of *Lecture Notes in Computer Science*, pages 170–
              186. Springer, 2007.

[Har97]   Heather Harreld. Government debates new encryption standard.
              Federal Computer Week, 1997. March 30.

[Hås01]   Johan Håstad. Some optimal inapproximability results. *J. ACM*,
              48(4):798–859, 2001.

[HG07]   Nick Howgrave-Graham. A hybrid lattice-reduction and meet-in-
              the-middle attack against NTRU. In *Advances in Cryptology – Crypto
              2007*, volume 4622/2007 of *Lecture Notes in Computer Science*, pages
              150–169. Springer, 2007.

[HGNP+03]   Nick Howgrave-Graham, Phong Q. Nguyen, David Pointcheval,
              John Proos, Joseph H. Silverman, Ari Singer, and William Whyte. The
              impact of decryption failures on the security of NTRU encryption. In
              Advances in Cryptology – Crypto 2003, volume 2729/2003 of *Lecture
              Notes in Computer Science*. Springer, 2003.

[HKM95]   Carlo Harpes, Gerhad Kramer, and James Massey. A generaliza-
              tion of linear cryptanalysis and the applicability of Matsui's piling-up
              lemma. In *Advances in Cryptology – Eurocrypt '95*, volume 473/1995
              of *Lecture Notes in Computer Science*, pages 24–39. Springer, 1995.

[HMU01]   J. Hopcroft, R. Motwani, and J. Ullman. *Introduction to Automata The-
              ory, Languages, and Computation*. Pearson Addison Wesley, 2001.

[HPS98]   Jeffrey Hoffstein, Jill Pipher, and Joseph H. Silverman. NTRU: A ring-based public key cryptosystem. In *Algorithmic Number Theory*, volume 1423/1998 of *Lecture Notes in Computer Science*. Springer, 1998.

[HPS01]   Jeffrey Hoffstein, Jill Pipher, and Joseph H. Silverman. NSS: An NTRU lattice-based signature scheme. In *Advances in Cryptology – Eurocrypt 2001*, volume 2045/2001 of *Lecture Notes in Computer Science*. Springer, 2001.

[HS00]   Holger H. Hoos and Thomas Stützle. SATLIB: An online resource for research on SAT. In *Third Workshop on the Satisfiability Problem (SAT 2000)*, pages 283–292. IOS Press, 2000. see also http://www.satlib.org.

[ILL89]   R. Impagliazzo, L. Levin, and M. Luby. Pseudorandom generation from one-way functions. In *Proceedings 21st ACM Symposium on Theory of Computation*, pages 12–24. ACM Press, 1989.

[IM03]   Russell Impagliazzo and Sara Miner. Anonymous credentials with biometrically-enforced non-transferability. In *Proceedings of the 2003 ACM Workshop on Privacy in the Electronic Society*, pages 60–71. ACM, 2003.

[IR89]   R. Impagliazzo and S. Rudich. Limits on the provable consequences of one-way permutations. In *Proceedings of 21st Annual ACM Symposium on the Theory of Computing*, pages 44–61, 1989.

[Jud07]   Peter Judge. Technology: Computers are about to take a quantum leap into the future: Scientists claim to have a breakthrough that will revolutionise computing. *The Guardian*, page 3, February 8, 2007.

[KLC+00]   Ki Hyoung Ko, Sang Jin Lee, Jung Hee Cheon, Jae Woo Han, Ju-sung Kang, and Choonsik Park. New public-key cryptosystem using braid groups. In *Advances in Cryptology - Crypto 2000*, volume 1880/2000 of *Lecture Notes in Computer Science*. Springer, 2000.

[Knu98]   Donald E. Knuth. *Sorting and Searching*, volume 3 of *The Art of Computer Programming*. Addison-Wesley, second edition, 1998.

[Koz92]   Dexter Kozen. *The Design and Analysis of Algorithms*. Texts and Monographs in Computer Science. Springer, 1992.

[Koz06]   Dexter Kozen. *Theory of Computation*. Texts in Computer Science. Springer, 2006.

[KPG99]   Aviad Kipnis, Jacques Patarin, and Louis Goubin. Unbalanced oil and vinegar signature schemes. In *Advances in Cryptology EUROCRYPT 99*, volume 1592/1999 of *Lecture Notes in Computer Science*, pages 206–222, 1999.

[KS99]   Aviad Kipnis and Adi Shamir. Cryptanalysis of the HFE public key cryptosystem by relinearization. In *Advances in Cryptology – Crypto '99*, volume 1666/1999 of *Lecture Notes in Computer Science*, pages 19–30. Springer, 1999.

[KZ97]   Howard J. Karloff and Uri Zwick. A 7/8-approximation algorithm for MAX 3SAT. In *Proceedings of the 38th Annual Symposium on Foundations of Computer Science (FOCS '97)*, pages 406–415. IEEE Computer Society, 1997.

[LLK+06]   Xiangdong Li, Lin Leung, Andis Chi-Tung Kwan, Xiaowen Zhang, Dammika Kahanda, and Michael Anshel. Post-quantum key exchange protocols. *Proceedings of the International Society for Optical Engineering*, 6244, 2006. arXiv:quant-ph/0603230v3.

[LM91a]   Xuejia Lai and James Massey. Markov ciphers and differential cryptanalysis. In *Advances in Cryptology – Eurocrypt '91*, volume 547/1991 of *Lecture Notes in Computer Science*, pages 17–39. Springer, 1991.

[LM91b]   Xuejia Lai and James Massey. A proposal for a new block encryption standard. In *Advances in Cryptology – Eurocrypt '90*, volume 473/1991 of *Lecture Notes in Computer Science*, pages 389–405. Springer, 1991.

[Lyn96]   Nancy A. Lynch. *Distributed Algorithms*. Morgan Kaufmann Publishers, 1996.

[Mas94]   James Massey. SAFER K-64: A byte-oriented block-ciphering algorithm. In *Fast Software Encryption 1993*, volume 809/1994 of *Lecture Notes in Computer Science*. Springer, 1994.

[Mat94]   Mitsuru Matsui. Linear crypatanalysis method for DES cipher. In *Eurocrypt '93 – Advances in Cryptology*, volume 765/1994 of *Lecture Notes in Computer Science*, pages 286–397. Springer, 1994.

[Mer82]   Ralph C. Merkle. *Secrecy, authentication, and public key systems*. UMI Research Press, 1982.

[Mer88]   Ralph C. Merkle. A digital signature based on a conventional encryption function. In *Advances in Cryptology – Crypto '87*, volume 293/1988 of *Lecture Notes in Computer Science*. Springer, 1988.

[MGK06]   Robert Mingesz, Zoltan Gingl, and Laszlo B. Kish. Johnson(-like)-noise-Kirchhoff-loop based secure classical communicator demonstrated for ranges of two kilometers to two thousand kilometers, 2006. arXiv.org:physics/0612153.

[MH78]   Ralph Merkle and Martin Hellman. Hiding information and signatures in trapdoor knapsacks. *IEEE Transactions on Information Theory*, IT-24(5):525–530, September 1978.

[MI83]   Tsutomu Massumoto and Hideki Imai. A class of asymmetric cryptosystems based on polynomials over finite rings. In *1983 IEEE International Symposium on Information Theory*. IEEE, 1983.

[Mic01]   Daniele Micciancio. Improving lattice based cryptosystems using the hermite normal. In *Cryptography and Lattices : International Conference, CaLC 2001*, volume 2146/2001 of *Lecture Notes in Computer Science*, pages 126–145. Springer, 2001.

[Mic07]   Daniele Micciancio. Cryptographic functions from worst-case complexity assumptions. In *LLL+25*, 2007.

[MOV93]   A.J. Menezes, T. Okamoto, and S.A. Vanstone. Reducing elliptic curve logarithms to logarithms in a finite field. *IEEE Transactions on Information Theory*, 39:1639–1646, September 1993.

[MR02]   Sean Murphy and Matthew Robshaw. Essential algebraic structure with the AES. In *Advances in Cryptology – Crypto 2002*, volume 2442/2002 of *Lecture Notes in Computer Science*, pages 1–16. Springer, 2002.

[MR04]   Daniele Micciancio and Oded Regev. Worst-case to average-case reductions based on gaussian measures. In *45th Annual IEEE Sympo-suim on Foundations of Computer Science (FOCS 2004)*, pages 372–361. IEEE, 2004.

[MSU06]   Alexei Myasnikov, Vladimir Shpilrain, and Alexander Ushakov. Random subgroups of braid groups: an approach to cryptanalysis of a braid group based cryptographic protocol. In *Proceedings of the 9th International Conference on Theory and Practice of Public-Key Cryptography (PKC 2006)*, volume 3958/2006 of *Lecture Notes in Computer Science*. Springer, 2006.

[MvOV97]   Alfred Menezes, Paul C. van Oorschot, and Scott Vanstone. *Handbook of Applied Cryptography*. CRC Press, 1997.

[Nat99]   National Institute of Standards and Technology. FIPS 46-3 Data Encryption Standard, October 1999.

[Ngu05]   L. Nguyen. Accumulators from bilinear pairings and applications to id-based ring signatures and group membership revocation. In *CT-RSA 2005*, volume 2005/3376 of *Lecture Notes in Computer Science*, pages 275–292. Springer, 2005.

[NR06]   Phong Nguyen and Oded Regev. Learning a parellelepiped: Cryptanalysis of ggh and ntru signatures. In *Advances in Cryptology – Eurocrypt 2006*, volume 4004/2006 of *Lecture Notes in Computer Science*, pages 271–388, 2006.

[OA94]   Kazuo Ohta and Kazumaro Aoki. Linear cryptanalysis of the fast data encipherment algorithm. In *Advances in Cryptography – Crypto*

'94, volume 839/1994 of *Lecture Notes in Computer Science*, pages 12–17. Springer, 1994.

[O'C95]   Luke O'Connor. On the distribution of characteristics in bijective mappings. In *Journal of Cryptology*, volume 8, pages 67–86. Springer, March 1995.

[Odl90]   A. M. Odlyzko. The rise and fall of the knapsack cryptosystems. In *PSAM: Proceedings of the 42nd Symposium in Applied Mathematics*, pages 75–88, 1990.

[OTU00]   Tatsuaki Okamoto, Keisuke Tanaka, and Shigenori Uchiyama. Quantum public-key cryptosystems. In *Advances in Cryptology - Crypto 2000*, volume 1880/2000 of *Lecture Notes in Computer Science*. Springer, 2000.

[Pap95]   Christos H. Papadimitriou. *Computational Complexity*. Addison-Wesley, 1995.

[Pat96]   Jacques Patari. Hidden fields equations (HFE) and isomorphisms of polynomials (IP): Two new families of asymmetric algorithms. In *Advances in Cryptology – Eurocrypt '96*, volume 1070/1996 of *Lecture Notes in Computer Science*, pages 33–48. Springer, 1996.

[Pat97]   Jacques Patarin. The oil and vinegar signature scheme. In *Dagstuhl Workshop on Cryptography*, September 1997.

[PJH03]   Seong-Hun Paeng, Bae Eun Jung, and Kil-Chan Ha. A lattice based public key cryptosystem using polynomial. In *Public Key Cryptogra-*

phy - PKC 2003, volume 2567/2003 of *Lecture Notes in Computer Science*, pages 292–308. Springer, 2003.

[PNRB94]   Bart Preneel, Marniz Nuttin, Vincent Rijmen, and Johan Buelens. Cryptanalysis of the CFB mode of the DES with a reduced number of rounds. In *Advances in Cryptology – Crypto '93*, volume 773/1994 of *Lecture Notes in Computer Science*, pages 212–224. Springer, 1994.

[PS08]   Xavier Pujol and Damien Stehlé. Rigorous and efficient short lattice vectors enumeration. In *Advances in Cryptology - Asiacrypt 2008*, 2008. Publication pending.

[Rab83]   Michael Rabin. Transaction protection by beacons. *Journal Computer and System Sciences*, 27(2):256–267, October 1983.

[Reg04]   Oded Regev. New lattice-based cryptographic constructions. *Journal of the ACM*, 51(6):899–942, November 2004.

[Reg06]   Oded Regev. Lattice-based cryptography. In *Advances in Cryptology - CRYPTO 2006*, volume 4117/2006 of *Lecture Notes in Computer Science*, pages 131–141, 2006.

[RJ04]   James Risen and David Johnston. The reach of war: The offense; Chalabi reportedly told Iran that U.S. had code. *The New York Times*, 2004. June 2.

[RSA78]   R. Rivest, A. Shamir, and L. Adleman. A method for obtaining digital signatures and public key cryptosystems. *Communications of the ACM*, 21(2):120–126, Feb. 1978.

[RSN+01]   Andrew Rukhin, Juan Soto, James Nechvatal, Miles Smid, Elaine Barker, Stefan Leigh, Mark Levenson, Mark Vangel, David Banks, Alan Heckert, James Dray, and San Vo. A statistical test suite for random and pseudorandom number generators for cryptographic applications, May 2001. NIST Special Publication 800-22.

[Rud88]   Steven Rudich. *Limits on the Provable Consequences of One-way Functions*. PhD thesis, EECS Department, University of California, Berkeley, 1988.

[Sch93]   Bruce Schneier. Description of a new variable-length key, 64-bit block cipher (Blowfish). In *Fast Software Encryption, (FSE '93)*, pages 191–204. Springer-Verlag, 1993.

[Sch96]   Bruce Schneier. *Applied Cryptography*. Wiley, second edition, 1996.

[Sha48]   Claude E. Shannon. A mathematical theory of communication. *Bell Telephone System Technical Publications*, 1948.

[Sha49]   Claude Shannon. *Communication Theory and Secrecy Systems*. John Wiley and Sons, 1949. `http://netlab.cs.ucla.edu/wiki/files/shannon1949.pdf`.

[Sha84]   Adi Shamir. A polynomial time algorithm for breaking the basic Merkle-Hellman cryptosystem. *IEEE Transactions on Information Theory*, IT-30(5):699–704, September 1984.

[Sho94]   Peter Shor. Algorithms for quantum computation: discrete logarithms and factoring. In *Proceedings of the 35th Annual Symposium on Foundations of Computer Science*, pages 124–134. IEEE, 1994.

[Sil99]   J. Silverman. Estimated breaking times for NTRU lattices. Technical Report 12, NTRU Cryptosystems, 1999.

[Sin06]   Carston Sinz. SAT-Race 2006, 2006. International Conference on Theory and Applications of Satisfiability Testing (SAT06), See also: `http://fmv.jku.at/sat-race-2006/`.

[SKW⁺98]   Bruce Schneier, John Kelsey, Doug Whiting, David Wagner, and Chris Hall. On the Twofish key schedule. In *Fifth Annual Selected Areas in Cryptography (SAC '98)*, volume 1556/1999 of *Lecture Notes in Computer Science*, 1998.

[SM88]   Akihiro Shimizu and Shoji Miyaguchi. Fast data encipherment algorithm FEAL. In *Advances in Cryptology – Eurocrypt '87*, volume 304/1988 of *Lecture Notes in Computer Science*, pages 267–281. Springer, 1988.

[SP00]   Peter W. Shor and John Preskill. Simple proof of security of the BB84 quantum key distribution protocol. *Phys. Rev. Lett.*, 85(2):441–444, Jul 2000.

[Sti02]   Douglas Stinson. *Cryptography: Theory and Practice*. Chapman and Hall, 2002.

[Szy04]   Michael Szydlo. Merkle tree traversal in log space and time. In *Advances in Cryptology – Eurocrypt 2004*, volume 3027/2004 of *Lecture Notes in Computer Science*, pages 541–554. Springer, 2004.

[Tod89]   S. Toda. On the computational power of *PP* and ⊕*P*. In *Proceedings of the 30th Symposium of the Foundations of Computer Science (FOCS '89)*, pages 514–519. IEEE, 1989.

[Vau01]   Serge Vaudenay. Cryptanalysis of the Chor-Rivest cryptosystem. *Journal of Cryptology*, 14(2):87–100, January 2001.

[VV85]   L.G. Valiant and V.V. Vazirani. *NP* is as easy as detecting unique solutions. In *Proceedings of the 17th ACM Symposium on Theory of Computing (STOC '85)*, pages 458–463. ACM, 1985.

[Wat06]   John Watrous. Zero knowledge against quantum attacks. In *Proceedings of the 38th Annual ACM Symposium on Theory of Computing (STOC '06)*, pages 296–315. ACM Press, 2006.

[Way93]   Peter Wayner. Content-addressable search engines and DES-like systems. In *Advances in Cryptology – Crypto '92*, volume 740/1993 of *Lecture Notes in Computer Science*, pages 575–587. Springer, 1993.

[Wie83]   Stephen Wiesner. Conjugate coding. *ACM SIGACT News*, 15(1):78–88, 1983.

[YT95]   Amr M. Youssef and Stafford E. Tavares. Resistance of balanced S-boxes to linear and differential cryptanalysis. *Information Processing Letters*, 56(5):249–252, 1995.

Index

maxreject, 85–87

access control lists, 98
algorithm
  3SAT distributed, 88
  Avalanche security experiment, 53
  Correlation security experiment, 49
  differential analysis, 54
  Dragonfire encryption, 64
  Pineapple encryption, 42
avalanche effect, 24

balanced, 25
braid groups, 14

cipher
  Feistel, 24
  iterated, 23–24
  polymorphic, 58
ciphers
  AES, 21
  block, 30
  Blowfish, 21
  DES, 20
  Dragonfire, 22, 57–68, 72
  FEAL, 18
  Feistel, 35–36
  GGH, 15–16
  GOST 28147, 20–21
  IDEA, 18–20
  knapsack, 13–14
  Matsumoto-Imai cryptosystem, 15
  NTRU, 14
  Pineapple, 41–52, 71–72
  Rijndael, 21
  SAFER, 22

Twofish, 21–22
ciphers:evolution, 19
class, 26
complete (cipher), 24
complexity class, 26
  #P, 28–29, 96
  A.M., 29
  complement, 27
  complete, 28
  NP, 27
  P, 27
  PH, 27–28, 96
  PSPACE, 28
  RP, 96
complexity of cryptography, 6–8
  symmetric-key ciphers, 34–35
compromised, 24–25
confuse, 24
cryptanalysis, 39
  algebraic, 40–41
  bilinear, 40
  differential, 39–40, 50, 55
  linear, 40
cryptovariable, 24–25

diffuse, 24
digital credentials, 76–77, 97
digital timestamping, 98–99

elections, 84–85, 88
experiment
  Avalanche, 49–50, 53, 54
  Correlation, 47–49

generic complexity, 8–10, 14

Hamming distance, 50
hidden field equations, 14–15

key scheduling, 58–68

language, 26

negative database, 16

Oil-Vinegar schemes, 15
one-way accumulators, 76
one-way permutations, 6–8
oracles, 29

polymorphic S-boxes, 58
polymorphism, 58
polynomially bounded, 27
polynomially-bounded, 27
post-quantum systems, 78
problem
    SAT, 74–75
    3SAT, 77–78, 80, 94–95
    USAT, 96
    closest vector problem, 15–16
    conjugacy decomposition, 14
    counting, 28–29, 96
    discrete log, 10
    factoring, 10
    generalized conjugacy search, 14
    knapsack, 13–14
    lattice reduction, 15–16
    set membership, 73–74
pseudo-independence, 65–68
pseudorandom number generators, 34,
        68–71

quantum, 10–13
    cryptography, 16
    Grover's Search Algorithm, 11–13
    Shor's Algorithm, 10

randomness tests, 69–70
reducible, 28

S-Box, 24

S-box, 24
set membership, 78–87

thermal noise, 16
Turing machine, 25–26
    alternating, 26
    decides, 26
    deterministic, 25–26
    nondeterministic, 25–26
    oracle, 26
    probabilistic, 26
    simulates, 26

Zero knowledge, 29

Vita

Michael de Mare was born in Brooklyn, New York on October 14, 1969. He has a Bachelor of Science from Clarkson University in Computer Science awarded May 1991, a Master of Science from State University of New York Institute of Technology in Computer Science awarded December 2004, and is a doctoral candidate at Stevens Institute of Technology in Computer Science. He is currently a Visiting Instructor of Computer Science at State University of New York Institute of Technology. He worked as a systems analyst at Giordano Automation from 1992 to 1994, as a senior software engineer at Ikos Systems from 1994 through 1995, for Technoproductions Inc. (consulting for Ikos Systems) from 1996 through 1998, and as a senior software engineer at LSI Logic from 1998 through 2000. His publications include *Efficient Broadcast Timestamping*, a technical report at Clarkson University, [BdM91], *One-Way Accumulators: A Decentralized Approach to Digital Signatures* at Eurocrypt '93, [BdM94] and *Secure Set Membership Using* 3SAT at the Eighth International Conference on Information and Communications Security (ICICS 2006), [dMW06], as well as his masters thesis: *An Analysis of Certain Cryptosystems and Related Mathematics*, [dM04] and the patent application: *Iterative Symmetric-Key Ciphers With Keyed S-boxes Using Modular Exponentiation*, [dM08]. He was a National Merit Scholar Letter of Commendation winner and won an Engineering Excellence Award at LSI Logic.

www.ingramcontent.com/pod-product-compliance
Lightning Source LLC
Chambersburg PA
CBHW080422060326

40689CB00019B/4343